Praise for *Helping Yourself With*

(an earlier edition of **Herbs Their Clin**

"... a serious and enjoyable introduction to the subject ... recommended for public library purchase."
Small Press The Magazine for Independent/In-House/Desktop Publishing

"Fascinating reading ... readers interested in alternative therapies will want to investigate this volume."
The American Library Assocation *Booklist*

"... a self-help guide that explains herbal remedies and tells you what vitamins and minerals can do for a healthy lifestyle."
Health Review magazine

"... a good guide for using already available preparations."
American Herb Association Newsletter

and other books by Dr. Terry Willard

Edible and Medicinal Plants of the Rocky Mountains

"As I look through this book, I find the stuff I want to know. I find the hand of an experienced pro, who knows the plants personally, has had dirty hand, and a sore back, gotten sore eyes from searching the abstracts, understands the chemistry ... Thanks Terry, I don't have to live a couple of decades in the North Country to learn the plants the way I want to. I have this book."
Michael Moore
Author of *Medicinal Plants of the Mountain West*
and *Medicinal Plants of the Desert and Canyon West*

Reishi Mushroom: Herb of Spiritual Potency and Medical Wonder

"The awareness of Reishi mushrooms as examples of the role that Chinese medicinal mushrooms can offer to public health is just beginning. This timely book will accelerate that trend."
Herbalgram
The Journal of the American Botanical Council and
Herb Research Foundation

"This book provides a thorough referenced introduction for both the scientist and non-scientist alike."
Foster's Botanical & Herb Reviews

Textbook of Modern Herbology (Second Edition)

" ... definitely beyond the class of popular herbals that have been offered over the last few years. A good book!"

Michael Tierra, C.A., N.D.
Author of *The Way of Herbs* and *Planetary Herbology*

"I was amazed at the amount of information, and ease of referencc ... credible, scientific yet practical. I'm not easily impressed by books, but I don't want to do without this one."

Tracey Cochrane
Editor, *Vitamin Supplement Journal*

"Good textbook. Thank you for your contribution to the [Herbal] Renaissance."

James Green
Professor, California School of Herbal Studies

The Wild Rose Scientific Herbal (Second Edition)

"... an exciting book in concept and execution. Dr. Willard reveals his deep understanding and working knowledge of botanical medicine and exemplifies the alchemical approach in this work by providing a full-spectrum presentation of each medicinal plant."

Mitch Stargrove, N.D.
Professor, Oregon College of Oriental Medicine and
National College of Naturopathic Medicine

The Textbook of Advanced Herbology

"The author blends Western chemical pharmacology with Asian traditional medicine ... an interesting and richly packed work that is appropriate for advanced students."

Mark Blumenthal
Editor, *Herbalgram*, Journal of the American Botanical Council

" ... the book blends pharmacology and modern scientific research with ancient traditions, working towards a balance of Eastern and Western philosophies ... an excellent reference book for any professional herbalist."

Anne McIntyre, N.I.M.H., U.K.
Journal of Herbal Medicine

"... connect the 'mind' of scientific understanding with the 'soul' of traditional medicine ... a simple understanding of the plant constituents in a biochemical way — brings in clinical experience and traditional medical thought"

from the Foreword by Christopher Hobbs, L.Ac.
Author of *Echinacea: The Immune Herb*
and *Medicinal Mushrooms: An Exploration of Tradition, Healing, & Culture*

Herbs

Their Clinical Uses

by
Terry Willard, Ph.D.

Wild Rose College of Natural Healing, Ltd.
400, 1228 Kensington Rd. N.W.
Calgary, Alberta
T2N 4P9

Publisher's Note: Individuals seeking relief from illness should consult a qualified health practitioner. This book cannot, and is not meant to, replace the services of a health professional.

Some materials in this publication appeared under the titles *Feeling Good with Natural Remedies* and *Helping Yourself with Natural Remedies*.

Library of Congress Cataloguing-in-Publication Data

Willard, Terry, 1951-
Herbs Their Clinical Uses

Includes Index
1. Herbs-- Therapeutic use. 2. Medicine -- Formulae, receipts, prescription.
3. Therapeutics, Physiological.
I. Title
RM666.H33W55 1996 615'321 86-9714
ISBN 0-9691727-7-x

Wild Rose College of Natural Healing, Ltd.
400, 1228 Kensington Rd. N.W.
Calgary, Alberta, CANADA
T2N 4P9
Phone: (403) 270-0936
FAX: (403) 283-0799

ISBN 0-9691727-7-x

Printed in the United States of America

Dedication

This book is first dedicated to my three teenagers, Juniper, Yarrow and Aiyana. Even though teenagers can be a handful for a single parent with a busy schedule, I love them dearly. Thanks for giving me the space to redo this book. From the best "disker" in the house.

Second, I have to dedicate this book to James McCormick, for all the help in bringing another project to fruition and being a friend through tough times.

Third, I would like to dedicate this book to the Deva of Wild Rose for continuing to amaze me with the challenges and rewards it has put in front of me and my staff in the service of those needing it, sick or well!

Fourth, I would like to make a dedication to all of the patients that have given me the knowledge to write this book. Without your comments and feedback, I would not have learned so much with such practical value.

Acknowledgements

A complete list of acknowledgements would be impossible. It would include all the lecturers I have heard, all books I have read, people I meet in my day-to-day-life and, most of all, the patients I have seen in the past.

A list of people working solely on the earlier versions of this book will have to suffice:

Illana Holloway, for suggesting the book and prodding me on. Don Hobsbawn, editing, arranging and paste ups. Penny Hess/Skylark, word processing, editing, and patience. Marie Gagnon, word processing. Dr. Ross Skaken, Foreword. Henry Garand, editing. Steve Burger, technical editing. Dorothy Caldwell for encouragement and time to work on this book. Rose Danby, for editing diagrams and artwork. Blaine Andrusek, cover photography. Donna Shannon, editing and promotion. James McCormick, last-minute editing and production.

Second Printing: Donna Shannon and James McCormick.

For this Revised Edition:

Again, the most important person helping to create this book was James McCormick. His dedication and hard work (even working through Christmas) has made this possible. I owe him more than words can express.

Editing and read-throughs were done by Dorothy Caldwell, Elaine Codling and Mary Teresa Kelly. Again, Blaine Andrusek, did a outstanding job on the cover photo. Great support and suggestions were given by Elliot Balbert, Cal Bewicke, Cheryl Richitt, Lisa Rostalki and Stacey Weinstein.

Foreword

As one becomes familiar with the philosophy of health and healing, two principles emerge which dominate the basic biological functions of the human organism in health and disease. The first is that the health or harmony of body, mind and soul are so closely interrelated that it is rare that any treatment of lasting value considers only the treatment of one of these aspects, without giving some attention to the other two.

The second premise is that for every human ill there are remedies to be found in nature, present in the fruit, herbs, seeds and creatures on this earth.

More and more we are learning that this first concept of man is an entity that functions on several interrelated levels of being. The second premise, which invites an exploration of natural healing methods, is the subject of this book.

Hippocrates, the father of modern medicine, stated: "Let your food be your medicine, let your medicine be your food.".

When we examine the preconditions, principal factors and forces which create, sustain and evolve life on our planet, we find them to be: atmosphere (air), hydrosphere (water), cosmosphere (solar and other cosmic radiations whose nature we do not yet fully know), lithosphere (the earth's crust with its chemical elements) and the botanosphere (steppes with the grasses, the different seed-bearing plants, the forests and trees, especially trees with fruits). These are the factors, the forces, the preconditions of the appearance of the evolution and of the maintenance of life. We have a heredity which scientists call "ontogenetic experience" in the organism. These factors have a very important hereditary influence on our organism.

Our Twentieth Century technology is able to harness these energies in their natural state as well as their products and processes in tablets, tinctures, fluid extracts, special preparations that concentrate by pre-infusion and potentizing (homeopathic method).

The author has had more than two decades of clinical application and experience in the use of these energies in the form of vitamins, minerals and herbs. He lectures to health professionals as well as to the public throughout Canada, the United States and Europe.

I am confident you will find this book of great value in your life and the lives of your family.

Dr. Ross Skaken, B.A., N.D., F.A.C.A.C.N.

Table of Contents

Introduction

Did you ever notice on a bus, at a party or at your place of work that most people don't have a smile on their faces? Did you ever notice in yourself or others around you that by the end of the work day you really don't have that much energy left to do some of those personal or family things you really would like to do? A lot of people are walking around only partly "energized" as there seems to be something continuously draining them. Well, that is what this book is about: trying to use some simple methods to make you healthy enough to feel good at the end of the day.

In looking at some of the most common ailments encountered by the average family, you will be presented with natural remedies that have helped people over the centuries as well as some of the most current research information. These remedies are generally without side effects (except where noted) and as is explained in the section "Herbal Philosophy," they support the body with energy instead of "stealing" it.

By using these methods, combined with some personal observation and adjustment, we can work on our bodies in a natural way and perhaps gain that extra "plus": feeling good!

In writing this book I've tried to keep it as simple as possible by using easy-to-understand language and easily obtainable herbs, herbal formulas and supplements.

It should be remembered at all times that you have to deal with a person as a whole individual, not just as separate parts. We seldom have just one little thing wrong with us. We are a complex mixture of mental, emotional, spiritual and physical attributes, and as such, everything has to be considered. The physical body alone is a very complex mechanism. For example, you can't have a liver problem without it affecting the rest of the body. The blood will not be cleansed properly, the kidneys and skin will be burdened by the elimination of toxins, and the digestive system will suffer from lack of proper bile production.

Consider this writing as an information base and use it as a guideline only, as it is not meant to replace the Health Practitioner. It should not be used as a self-prescribing book. The information is set out to help you understand how the various herbs can work, especially in complex herbal formulas where one herb's interaction with the next expands the quality of the whole so as to be much more than the sum of the individual parts -- 'Synergy'. Herbs are one of the most important forms of medicine and food, having a long history as tested cures. Even today, in the Twentieth Century, more people worlds wide are being treated daily with herbs than with any other modality of medicine. This is something we often forget, living on our isolated continent of North America.

It should be understood that herbs work synergistically with vitamins, minerals and other therapeutic modalities and are usually more effective when used together.

Let's go on to the practical aspects of this book!

How to use this book

This book is set up in five sections:

1. Herbal Philosophy: understanding the energy of herbs.
2. Herbal and Synergistic Formulas.
3. Encyclopedia of Ailments and Treatments.
4. Appendices.
5. Cross-reference index.

The first section of the book gives the reader an understanding of herbs, their energy, and their differences from pharmaceuticals. It deals with the essence of why herbs should be used, along with some guidelines for choosing and preparing them.

The second section deals with many of the formulas found in the encyclopedic section. These are the formulas that I prefer and use regularly in my practice. Some I have formulated myself, and some have been formulated by other herbalists both modern and traditional. Most of the formulas are in a marketable form, meaning that they should be easily obtainable in your local health food store or through a health practitioner.

The formula section should be continually cross-referenced to the encyclopedic section for determining the best formulas and dosages to be used in the various situations.

The third and largest section of the book is the encyclopedia of ailments. This should be used as a reference and is most effective when cross-referenced with the formulas section and appendices. Each reference is in several parts:

1. Description of the problem.
2. Recommended actions.
3. Single Herbs useful for the ailment.
4. Herbal Formulas that can be used.
5. Synergistic Vitamins and Minerals.

For some ailments I have also included suggested programs to follow and/or brief case studies.

Section four is one of the appendices covering diets, exercises and other procedures generally used throughout the encyclopedic section, including a glossary of terms you might not be familiar with.

Section five of the book is the index used to locate items not easily found in the encyclopedic section.

The encyclopedic order of the main body is for simplicity. The book was written in a workbook format with plenty of space for annotations. Use this space well and in future years I think you will find it very beneficial.

The Philosophy of Herbal Use

The most important issue in herbal use is why are they different? What is it that sets herbs apart from any other healing agent? To the herbalist, herbs are unique because they are not just a group of chemicals. Each herb has its own nature which, for want of better word, we call its personality. The concept of herbal personality is the basis of herbology and has played a major role in herb use for thousands of years.

Most of the world's people continue to use herbs as their primary form of medication. While various cultures may not have our knowledge of biochemistry of plants or the same perspective on the structure of the human body, all herb using cultures have an appreciation for the 'personality' of herbs. A herb is a living substance and has its own constellation of energy. We don't think of ourselves or our pet dog as being merely a conglomeration of physical parts. We have emotions, mental concepts and spiritual feelings.

It would be silly to assume that herbs don't have patterns of energy beyond mere molecules. North American Indians believe that the spirit of the herb is directly involved in a battle with an illness when herbal healing takes place. Other cultures (e.g., the Chinese and East Indian) choose their herbs by taste, smell and colour along with energies related to fire, metal, water, wood and earth - features which we might not think were important for healing. A first step in understanding herbology lies in appreciating the fact that we should focus just as much on the essence or 'personality' of the herb as on the scientific descriptions.

Alternative Perspectives in Medical Theory

Healing methods around the world take many approaches. The western medical philosophy we are most familiar with (medical doctors and allopathy) has generally taken a mechanical-scientific view towards health. If you have a broken arm, it can be splinted. If there is a missing chemical in a biochemical pathway, they can replace it or make a suitable piece to fit in. If some bacteria or viruses are present in your body, a powerful biochemical means can be found to destroy or subdue them. One must admit that western medical professionals are good mechanics who have helped many people, have tackled disease in powerful ways and can give us everything from artificial hearts to trauma care.

In our own past and around the world an alternative means of organizing medical care is known. This system starts with theories of life energy and relates it to the physical forms of human beings and diseases they have. Medicine in the traditions of European herbology, First Nations medicine, East Indian medicine and Chinese medicine is seen as the conscious manipulation of energy for healing the human body.

This energy is known by many names: the life force, chi, prana and also **vital energy**. Vital energy is the term which modern herbologists use because it is the purpose of non-allopathic medicine to keep this energy flowing correctly through the body or, if the flow is improper, to return it to its natural path. The herbalist feels that disease is caused by stagnant or incorrectly directed energy due to some energy blockage. The herbalist's role is not so much to attack a disease, but to maintain the natural flow of vital energy. The energy itself will rid the body of disease.

A Closer Look at Vital Energy

Vital Energy is the flow of energy through one's body. This can be likened to a river that gets unnaturally clogged or dammed, stopping the normal flow of its energy. The river forms a stagnant pool which, as I'm sure you've all seen, breeds abundant algae and insects in a swampy condition.

There are two very different ways to get rid of such things as mosquito larvae, abundant algae and other undesirables:

> 1. The way I was told in high school to get rid of mosquito larvae was to pour oil on the water so they couldn't breathe. You can also dump poisons into the water to make the environment unbearable for these organisms. Of course this also destroys most other life-supporting functions in the pond.
>
> 2. The other way is to work on dislodging the obstruction damming the river. This lets the river flow and cleans itself naturally.

Our bodies are quite similar to this river. Disease is the blocking of the natural vital energy that flows through our body. Let us say that at least some of these energy streams are the acupuncture lines in the body. When the energy is flowing properly along these pathways, it naturally keeps the body clean, just as the river does. Like a river, the bodily energy flow can handle a certain amount of waste.

To fight disease in our bodies, we can dump in all kinds of chemicals to make the environment unliveable for the intruder. We can, as an alternative, unplug the system and get the energy flowing again. As in the case of rivers, if these energy pathways are not obstructed and no wastes are put into them, the job of cleaning is not as taxing and the energy can then be used to support life.

Thus, our job is not to try to kill disease in our bodies. Our job is to keep the body free of energy obstruction so the natural vital energy flows throughout the body selecting, disintegrating, absorbing, assimilating and converting foodstuffs. In other words, we don't try to take on the role of trying to cure diseases; we merely assist the vital energy in our bodies to flow in an unobstructed way.

Herbs, in this sense, are not really considered medicines. They are just specialized foods which help vital energy flow, being somewhat selective in where their energy is directed. The 'personality' of the herb will be attracted to certain areas of the body similar to different types of people associating in like-minded' groups. For example, Juniper Berries have a 'personality' that strongly influences the kidneys.

This 'Vital Energy' is just one part of a modern herbalist's understanding of how herbs work. Understanding the chemical interactions the herbs have on the human physiological mechanism is just as significant. Most herbalists feel that one is fairly ineffective without the other. The "Vital Energy" of the herb is what makes it work. For something to work in a live biological system, it has to have life energy. Herbs, with their own life essence, work in harmony with the biological system to enact healing.

A pharmaceutical will copy the chemical makeup of a herb, but it can only work by overpowering the system, 'stealing' some of the body's life energy as it has none of its own. Pharmaceuticals are usually used when the body needs this life energy the most. In a medical crisis, for example, the pharmaceutical's power and fast action of the chemical are necessary. Of course, there may arise some side effects that have to be dealt with, but usually they can be best balanced out by herbal treatment later.

For the everyday non-critical health problems, herbals have a long proven history of cure. After all, most of the herbals we are dealing with have been tested on millions of people for thousands of years. Their methods of use have been very thoroughly studied.

The Ecology of Energy

The ecology of the energy that we use in our body, and for that matter, any biological system, is important to understand. We don't **really** eat because it tastes good or because it looks nice! The main reason for eating is to take energy into our body. All the food we eat is really little packets of energy that we use to animate ourselves, think or even read this page. We are a big nutritional factory that processes foodstuffs to give us energy, at least on the biological level. I eat an apple because it looks good, tastes good but more specifically because I need the energy it gives me. This energy is the Vital or biological energy that is in the food. Where does this energy come from?

The major energy source of our solar system is the sun, of course, and that is where our energy originates. Some 93 million miles away, the sun acts as a very efficient nuclear reactor, and produces untold amounts of energy. The planet Earth is fortunate in that it has developed a system for capturing this solar energy.

The Sun shines upon our planet where plants have the capability of capturing some of this energy, thus putting the energy into the biological system. Plants are the only biological system that can capture this solar energy to be used by the rest of the biological systems on this planet. One can easily see that the plant kingdom has a very important responsibility in being the sole collector of biological energy for our planet. It is also easy to see that the plant kingdom takes this responsibility very seriously, as plants seem completely dedicated to their job and the sun! If I have a potted plant in my window, it will bend toward the sun. If I turn the plant around it will switch its direction again orienting itself toward the sun. Of course it is impossible for us to consider what a plant might feel, but this level of complete dedication to the sun that the plants give almost seems like they 'feel' that the sun is their God. Could this be why some ancient human cultures conceived of the Sun as **their** God?

Looking at the situation a bit closer we can see what happens on a molecular level. When the Solar energy hits a chlorophyll molecule in the green parts of the plant, the Magnesium (Mg) atoms' electrons are excited. In the Magnesium atom the orbital of the electron expands. We could liken this to a person jumping for joy when something very exciting is happening. The plant, in its complete dedication, to the Sun seems to get very excited (or at least its Mg molecules do) when the radiation of the Sun shines upon it. This whole process is very simple, but is of the utmost importance, because this excitation of Magnesium represents the entrance of solar energy into the Earth's biological system. All other organisms live off this energy. Can we say then that the primary source of biological energy on our planet is the dedication that the plants have to the Sun? Some Alchemists believe that this is a good model to look at. If complete dedication is given to one's God, then all the energy necessary for existence will be given back.

This 'excited' energy is passed onto other molecules, such as ATP and $NADH_2$, for short - time storage in the plant cell. We can consider them solar batteries. This Solar energy, now converted to Biological energy is available to do work in the organism or to be stored in the form of nutrients such as a simple sugar called glucose. The basic energy manufacturing process of nature occurs through a series of chemical reactions, one of the best known being "the Krebs Cycle". If we now take two units of working energy and put it into the Krebs Cycle, with this basic stored energy, we get 38 units of working energy out on the other side of the reaction! This energy can be used elsewhere to make raw chemicals into various nutrients for the plant such as glycosides, alkaloids, vitamins and many other nutrients. The key point here is that it takes the excited energy of the original solar energy, being passed along the system, to activate these molecules. All of these biologically made nutrients have their molecules made up of excited electrons, energy from the original solar excitement of the magnesium molecule. Chemicals are basically shells that carry energy. We survive on biological energy. We have to eat living organisms with biological energy to survive. If this were not true, our lower jaws would be different, being more like a bulldozer for scooping up dirt, thus getting all of the minerals needed for the body. The plants do this for us; they pull the minerals out of the ground, filling them with live biological energy so that we can use them. Since eating is primariliy a need to obtain this biological energy, we eat plants, or organisms that eat plants.

To gain its energy a herbivore eats plants and a carnivore eats herbivores. To get our energy we can eat from any of these groups, as we are of a higher group. It is interesting to note that any waste materials, either in the form of excrements or parts not completely eaten, are recycled via the microorganisms. This compost makes it very much easier on the plants because now they do not have to convert all nutrients into biologically usable forms, since some nutrients absorbed from the soil are already in this form, and only need to get charged up.

Now what does all of this have to do with feeling good with natural remedies?

It is easy to see that to keep our solar batteries charged we need biological energy. What is most disease, but a lack of proper biological energy? When we are sick, we need certain types of nutrients to help heal us. These nutrients are really chemicals that are shells specific to our energy needs. Since we are looking more for the energy contained in the chemical than the shell itself we will normally be better served with chemicals that come from the biological realm.

Along come humans with isolated views of the universe. They look at the problem to make a "better" way. Looking at the way a plant makes a chemical that has traditionally been used for a certain health problem, people realize they can make it cheaper and faster, therefore making profits for themselves and their company. The big problem is that some pharmaceutical scientists don't realize that there is much more to plants and man than just chemicals. Man cannot live by chemicals alone. The only way that these chemicals can work in a biological system is to be activated by biological energy. Synthetic chemicals have to take the energy from the biological system they are in. These synthetic chemicals, which might be useful in crisis medicine, don't really have a place in our day to day life.

Synthetic chemicals, because of their lack of biological energy, have to be taken in fairly large quantities to work. Synthetic chemicals work like a bulldozer pushing chemicals down certain biochemical pathways. Since there are often side branches to these pathways a person often gets side effects from them. Herbs, on the other hand, have the biological energy already in them, so the same quantity of chemical is not needed to achieve the job. This has a threefold benefit:

> 1. Because the biological energy in the herb is in "harmony" with the biological needs of the body the herbal chemical most often goes down the right pathway without side effects.
>
> 2. We don't have the possibilities of as many side effects because of the lower quantity of chemical.

3. Biological energy is **given** to the body during this process, not **taken** as in the case of the synthetic chemical.

These benefits are not without any drawbacks though. Herbal energy takes much longer to work its benefits. Herbals are just not as fast as synthetic chemicals. This is why a smart herbalist will often surrender to a practitioner of synthetic chemicals in a crisis situation and then will try to clean up the side effects later.

A consumer has to make aware decisions of how to best help themselves and their family in disease situations. One must be able to decide between the synthetic way and the natural way. That is what this book is about. I have included the experience that I have obtained from more than 20 years of work with patients with various ailments. I have put it in an easy to understand format to be accessible to a large number of people. I hope you can benefit from that experience if the need arises.

There is still another major question to answer about herbs and that is: what form is best when taking herbs?

Method of Herbal Preparation

Herbs have traditionally been available in four forms: teas (infusions), capsules/tablets, fluid extracts and tinctures. Each form has its own advantage. Teas are valuable because the medicinal ingredients of the herb are in solution (menstruum), thereby allowing efficient absorption of the active ingredients. Capsules, on the other hand, are very convenient. They can be taken anytime and anywhere, and because the herb is encapsulated, its often unpalatable taste is shielded. Fluid extracts and tinctures are valuable because they are the most potent form of the herb. They also store for long periods of time, and because of their strength, small doses are as effective as larger doses of the same herb in another form.

However, each of these forms has its disadvantages. Medicinal teas are often unpalatable and inconvenient, requiring special preparation; therefore, people do not take them as often as they should. Encapsulated crude herbs, in spite of their remarkable convenience, are hard to digest because the active ingredients of the herb are entrapped within cellulose cages with no menstruum to release the essence. Only an optimally functioning digestive system (something we seldom see) can fully release them. Fluid extracts and tinctures taste, in a word, terrible and are messy. If they are not handled with caution, stained clothes are often the result. Teas, tinctures and fluid extracts throw away the bulk herb after extraction.

By extracting the herb and encapsulating it we can get the advantage of the whole herb, in a concentrated form and have the convenience of the 'pill' form. The big question is how do we concentrate it and what do we use as marker for the concentration. Each herb has a set of most active ingredients, by determining how much of these ingredients we desire, we can use this ingredient to create a guaranteed potency herb.

Guaranteed Potency (GP)

Guaranteed Potency is both a simple concept and a complicated procedure. As a practitioner of herbal medicine, one of the most important issues for me is the quality of the tools of my trade - the botanical materials that herbal formulas are based on. Just like the quality of wine varies from year to year, so do the quality of the herbs. It is possible these days, through sophisticated analytical techniques, such as High Performance Liquid Chromatography (HPLC) and other methods, to identify and measure the quantity of key biochemical constituents in various herbs. Upon analysis of some herbs like Cat's Claw, we can find as much as 1000% difference in the amounts of active ingredients. Goldenseal has shown 200-300% differences from one source to another. It is important as a practitioner to have good quality products. This is where guaranteed potency comes in. By knowing the quantity of the active ingredients we know how much to give a person. The idea of guaranteed potency is to produce a more effective product. This can be a fairly expensive procedure and not all herbs are suitable for the guaranteed potency approach, so we use a combination of guaranteed potency and raw material in producing formulas. Some herbs are suitable for concentration of the whole plant to give a more powerful and convenient product that is a good and safe medicine.

In this area, the Europeans are way ahead of the North Americans. They have researched and marketed a large variety of guaranteed potency single herbs. By blending the information they have with the tradition methods of creating herbal formulas, we can often come up with a superior product. Traditionally, a herbal formula has a master herb, with several 'helper' herbs. When possible I like to use a guaranteed potency herb for the master, giving them the strong support of other botanicals. In this way we combine the best of the herbal traditions and the confidence of using guaranteed botanical material. Of course, after all is said and done, you have to try the formula out in the clinic to see how it works. Formulas often look good on paper, but don't work as well in practice. Once in a while, the reverse is true. They work much better than one ever expected. The clinical formulas in this book are mostly those I have used for many years, so we know how they work.

The key in formulation is to combine guaranteed potency herbs with other useful herbs in a formula that has good clinical results. This process of guaranteed potency is quite different from standardization. Standardization is where you standardize everything to one ingredient, while guaranteed potency is concentration of the botanical, while keeping the active ingredients in ratios to the level desired. With standardization, you have to either "spike" the product, if the desired ingredient is too low, or take some away, if it is too high. With guaranteed potency we are working with the herb, concentrating it to a level that assures bioavailablity.

One important factor is faithfulness to current research and processing technology. This insures that key ratios of constituents are not disturbed. Guaranteed potency gives me the confidence that I'm using effective products as a wholistic practitioner.

Herbal And Nutritional Formulas

The following formulas are listed generically. Your health practitioner or health food store can help you find the single herbs, herbal combination or synergetic vitamin mineral products you need.

Guaranteed potency (GP) herbs are created using rigorous manufacturing methods. They should be used for the major ingredients of a formula whenever possible. For more information, see the section on guaranteed potency. In the following products you will often see that, where possible, the master herb of a formula is a guaranteed potency herb, denoted by a "GP".

Arthritis Formula

This herbal formula supports the body in dealing with arthritis or rheumatism by stopping swelling and inflammation and easing the pain in muscles and joints. While acting to reduce pain, it also aids in eliminating underlying toxins and metabolic problems that create arthritis.

Devil's Claw Extract (GP 1.5% Harpagosides) *Harpagophytum procumbens*
Yucca *Yucca sp.*
Chaparral *Larrea divaricata*
Red Clover Blossoms *Trifolium pratens*
Valerian root *Valerianna officinalis*

Devil's Claw Extract (GP 1.5% Harpagosides) and yucca are the most important herbal ingredients in Arthritis Formula. Both have a saponin-type chemical which acts similarly to cortisone. They have been shown to markedly reduce inflammation, while reportedly dissolving calcium deposits.

Red Clover and chaparral are both excellent alteratives, cleansing the system of excess toxicity and acidity, often an underlying cause of arthritic-related problems.

Valerian is an excellent nervine and is used to ease the pain associated with these problems.

Suggested Dosage Two to four capsules, two to four times a day depending on degree of problem. It is strongly suggested to follow an alkaline-forming diet (see Appendix).

Also consider Inflammation Ointment and Trauma Ointment

B and B Tincture

Black Cohosh *Cimicifuga racemosa*
Blue Cohosh *Caulophyllum thalictroides*
Blue Vervain *Verbena hastata*
Skullcap *Scutellaria lateriflora*
Lobelia *Lobelia inflata*
alcohol tincture with glycerine

B and B Tincture is a Dr J.R. Christopher formula. It is used mostly as an antispasmodic. It has been successfully employed for all kinds of spasms, including spastic colons, muscle spasms, hiccups and has even been used in cases of epilepsy.

Suggested Dosage 3-10 drops as needed, usually three times daily.

B complex (50)

B complex (50) is a complete range of B vitamins. B vitamins are essential as co-enzymes in many conversions of nutrients into energy. Deficiencies of the B complex can cause fatigue, depression, nervousness, sleep disturbance, loss of appetite, and nausea. Deficiencies of single B vitamins will have their own specific deficiency symptoms.

	Amount	US RDA %
Vitamin B_1 (Thiamine)	50 mg	3333%
Vitamin B_2 (Riboflavin)	50 mg	2941%
Vitamin B_6 (Pyridoxine)	50 mg	2500%
Vitamin B_{12} (Cobalamin)	50 mcg	833%
Niacinamide	50 mg	250%
Folic acid	400 mcg	100%
Biotin	50 mcg	17%
Pantothenic acid	50 mg	500%
Choline	50 mg	N/A
Inositol	50 mg	N/A
PABA	50 mg	N/A
in a base of UltraGreen	75 mg	N/A

(UltraGreen is a mixture of alfalfa, barley green, spirulina, parsley, spinach, peppermint and spearmint.)

Beta-CEZB$_6$

Beta-carotene	10,000 IU
Ester C	500 mg.
Echinacea	300 mg
Zinc gluconate	15 mg.
Vitamin B_6	50 mg.

This formula was originally meant to be an immune system prophylactic, but has come to play a much more central role in clinical practice. With the echinacea, ester C and beta-carotene, it is easy to see why it is employed for the immune system. We usually get a person who is at high risk of colds and flus (e.g., teachers, practitioners, service people, etc.) to take two of these tablets, twice daily going into the flu seasons (Fall and Spring). Many people feel that echinacea loses its immune potentiating quality if taken for more than twenty days. Both clinical experience and scientific studies have shown this is not true. As an immune prophylactic, we have found this formula to be very useful.

Many of the ingredients in this formula are beneficial for wound healing, and for the skin and connective tissue. This has lead to use of this formula in a much broader context: skin, eye issues, post-operative recovery and related health areas. Beta-carotene and vitamin C are well known as antioxidants, protecting the skin from the harshness of the sun. Several hormonal and reproductive functions are supported by vitamin C, vitamin B_6 and zinc.

Over the last several years I have found this formula to be a central tool of many of my therapies, as you will see reflected in the accompanying text about various health issues.

Suggested Dosage 2 tablets, twice daily or as directed by a health practitioner.

Bone, Flesh And Cartilage

Oak Bark *Quercus muhlenbergii*
Marshmallow Root *Althaea officinalis*
Mullein Herb *Verbascum thapsus*
Wormwood *Artemisia absinthium*
Lobelia *Lobelia inflata*
Skullcap *Scutellaria lateriflora*
Comfrey Root *Symphytum officinale*
Walnut Bark (or Leaves) *Juglans sp.*
Gravel Root *Eupatorium purpureum*

This is one of Dr J.R. Christopher's most famous formulas. To sum up this formula in a word, it is "magical". If anything is wrong with your bones, flesh or cartilage, this formula is of use. Use it on sprains, torn ligaments, bruises, breaks and a multitude of other connective tissue needs. It is also beneficial to take this same formula internally while applying it externally.

For a fomentation take the above formula and make into a strong tea (one tablespoon herbs or 1 tsp. of tincture to 1 cup boiled water and steep 20 minutes). Strain the tea and soak a piece of natural fiber material, such as cotton, in the tea. Lightly wring out the cloth and wrap it around the affected area. Cover with a plastic bag and then a towel. Apply twice daily for an hour if possible.

This formula can be made up in tincture form, using 1 tsp. of the tincture in hot water for the tea. It's just as effective as the fomentation. It also comes in the form of an ointment. The ointment is more convenient and is not quite as effective but it certainly does the job.

Taking this formula internally either in a tea or a capsule form will really support the effectiveness of the fomentation.

Suggested Dosage apply twice daily for an hour if possible. Drinking a cup of the tea daily will speed up the process.

Calcium/Magnesium

Calcium 500 mg
Magnesium 200 mg

Fruit base 540 mg
(Rose Hips, Cranberry, Raspberry, Strawberry, Orange, Bilberry, Grape skin and Pineapple)

Calcium/Magnesium is not "just another" simple calcium tablet. We recommend using Calcium/Magnesium derived from the Krebs Cycle (i.e., bound to essential organic acids like citrate, malate, fumarate, succinate and alpha-ketoglutarates). These have been shown to be the most assimilable by the human body and are recommended by most leading nutritionists.

Supplemental calcium/magnesium intake can be an important factor in preventing the development of osteoporosis (loss of bone minerals), usually in old age. It is also necessary for the growth and repair of many tissues in the body especially periodontal tissue and bone. They are also essential for nerve transmission function, cell membrane transport and neuromuscular activity.

The fruit base is included to supply a large variety of multiminerals and "mystery" factors, such as bioflavonoids, that support calcium/magnesium metabolism.

Suggested Dosage Three or four tablets daily, or as recommended by your health practitioner.

Cayenne Plus Formula

Cayenne (GP 90,000 Heat Units) *Capsicum fastigiatum*
Ginger root *Zingiber officinale*
Prickly Ash *Xanthoxylum sp.*
Virginia Snake Root *Aristolochia serpentaria*

Cayenne (GP 90,000 Heat Units) is considered one of our best stimulants, and is very effective in regulating blood pressure. At the core of this role is cayenne's ability to control cholesterol, both lowering plasma cholesterol and triglycerides. More importantly, it alters the LDL/HDL ratio. Cayenne decreases platelet aggregation and aids in thinning the blood. This herb is considered one of the great tonics. Ginger roots work as a peripheral stimulant, while reducing peripheral resistance and lowering cholesterol. Prickly Ash Bark is a strong direct (heart) stimulant giving heart support. Virginia Snake Root is also a direct (heart) tonic and blood circulation tonic.

Suggested Dosage 1-2 capsules, during two meals daily.

Cleansing Formula

The key actions of Cleansing Formula include cleansing the bloodstream, muscle and lymphatic system tissue of toxic waste material and metabolic by-products, and delivering these wastes out of the body via the urinary system. It has been recommended by many practitioners as an adjunct to fasting and other cleansing programs.

Red Clover and Chaparral are two of the strongest herbal alteratives known, and have been used successfully in many cases of cancer, heavy metal toxicity, lymphatic toxicity and mucous congestion.

Mullein and Marshmallow both work on the lymphatic system, soothing the mucous membranes specifically, while working as a demulcent throughout the whole system.
Uva Ursi and Parsley are diuretics which aid in collecting and eliminating excess body fluids through the urinary tract.

Burdock is an effective alterative, hepatic and tonic. Echinacea is alterative, diaphoretic and tonic.

Suggested Dosage One capsule a day for the first week. Increase by one capsule per day each week, until six capsules (two capsules, three times daily) are taken by the sixth week. This dosage is normally continued for six months.

Red Clover blossoms *Trifolium pratense*
Burdock root *Arctium lappa*
Echinacea leaves *Echinacea angustifolium*
Chaparral leaves *Larrea divaricata*
Mullein leaves *Verbascum thapsus*
Uva Ursi leaves *Arctostaphylos uva-ursi*
Parsley leaves *Petroselinum sativum*
Marshmallow root *Althaea officinalis*
Cascara Sagrada *Rhamnus purshiana*

Cleansing Tincture

This tincture is designed to provide a cleansing of the body with concentration on the urinary tract. Licorice root is considered the great detoxifier by the Chinese. Uva Ursi and Juniper berries are specific for the urinary tract, both toning and cleansing it. Cornsilk is an excellent mild diuretic that is soothing to the urinary tract. Yarrow works on cleansing the system, both through the urinary tract and as a diaphoretic that makes a person sweat more. Burdock is a cleanser with an especially positive effect on the liver. It has a building and purifying quality.

Suggested Dosage Twenty drops, twice daily

Licorice Root *Glycyrrhiza glabra*
Uva Ursi *Arctostaphylos uva-ursi*
Yarrow *Achillea millefolium*
Juniper berries *Juniperus communis*
Burdock Root *Arctium lappa*
Cornsilk *Zea mays*

Cranberry Concentrate Plus Formula

Cranberry Fruit extract
(GP 30% organic acids)
Vacinnium macrocarpum
Corn Silk *Zea mays*
Uva Ursi *Arctostaphylos uva-ursi*
Parsley Leaves
Petroselinum sativum

Cranberry juice has been used for centuries to stop kidney/bladder infections. The problem is that to make cranberries palatable, lots of sugar is usually added. Sugar can often encourage the inflammation. With cranberry concentrate, one can have the effect of cranberry juice without the negative effects of sugar or the bitter taste of straight cranberry juice. Several other herbs are added that are beneficial to the urinary tract.

Corn Silk is calming and soothing while possessing antimicrobial properties for the urinary tract. Uva Ursi has strong diuretic and antibiotic properties in the urinary tract, both cleansing and strengthening it. Parsley leaves are soothing and toning to the urinary tract.

Suggested Dosage 2 capsules, twice daily.

Curing Pills

Rhizoma Gastrodiae
Rhizoma Atractylodis
Flos Chrysanthemi
Radix Puerarae
Radix Trichosanthis
Radix Saussureae
Semen Coicis
Poria Cocos
Cortex Magnoliae Off.
Exocarpium Citr Rubrum
Herba Pogostemi
Radix Angelicae
Herba Mentha
She Chu
Fructus Oryzas Germinatus

"Curing Pills" is a famous Chinese formula. I know practitioners who claim that this formula has saved their lives. It may not have really saved their lives, but it certainly helped. Chinese herbalists recommend "Curing Pills" after a big feast when you know you have eaten too much. It will relieve gas and indigestion often accompanying big meals. "Curing Pills" is traditionally used for diarrhea, stomach upset, overindulgence of alcohol, and all gastrointestinal problems.

I have found it to be very useful for taking on trips into tropical areas, where one might pick up some not-so-friendly intestinal bacteria. We often suggest the use of Huang Lian Su (Berberini HCl, *Coptis sp.*) as a preventative, but Curing Pills if the prevention has not been sufficient.

Suggested Dosage one or two vials with some hot tea, one-six times daily. Or as needed.

Digestive Enzymes

Glutamic Acid HCl
Betaine HCl
Calcium ascorbate
Pancreatin N.F.
Bromelain 1:10
Papain

Digestive Enzymes is a capsulated formula of digestive enzymes and HCl (hydrochloric acid) that aids in digesting food. The capsule ensures that the various digestive aids can be specially prepared to be released in their proper environment: i.e., HCl (hydrochloric acid) in the stomach, and pancreatin in the duodenum.

Glutamic Acid HCl and Betaine HCl are two forms of hydrochloric acid that are properly buffered to aid in increasing stomach acidity for the first stages of protein digestion. Not only is HCl important for protein digestion, it is necessary to stimulate both hormone and digestive enzymes required in other digestive functions further down the digestive tract. Calcium Ascorbate is a salt form of Vitamin C that is also an excellent buffer for HCl in the stomach.

Pancreatin NF is a combination of pancreatin enzymes amylase, lipase and protease which are prepared to delay release until they reach the duodenum. These digestive enzymes aid in hydrolysing fats, digesting proteins and converting starch.

Bromelain and Papain are added for their well-known function of aiding digestion.

Suggested Dosage One or more capsules in the middle of the two major meals of the day or as directed by a health practitioner.

Echinacea Plus Formula

Echinacea purpurea (GP 4% Total Phenolic Compounds, 15% Echinacea Polysaccharides)
Echinacea angustifolium (GP 4% Total Phenolic Compounds, 15% Echinacea Polysaccharides)
Barberry *Berberis vulgaris*
Gold Thread *Coptis chinensis*
Missouri Snake Root *Parthenium integrifolium*
Licorice Root *Glycyrrhiza glabra*
Goldenseal Root *Hydrastis canadensis*

Echinacea species (GP 4% Total Phenolic Compounds, 15% Echinacea Polysaccharides) are well known for their immune-enhancing qualities, working both to prevent infection and to boost immune function after infection. Echinaceas have been shown to maintain the integrity of collagen matrices in connective tissue, thus slowing down the wrinkling and aging process. These two properties also give the echinaceas the ability of wound healing, while increasing recuperative powers after operations. By using the whole herb, of two species, along with the support herbs, we can enhance a wider spectrum of immune function.

Barberry, Gold Thread and Goldenseal roots all have antibiotic properties against a wide range of organisms including fungi, bacteria and viruses. They will strengthen the immune system, while improving the quality of the mucous membranes. Goldenseal is also considered the "King of the mucous membranes". Missouri Snake Root has been often mistaken for Echinacea in early research material, which showed it had great immuno-modulating properties similar to Echinacea. Licorice root is considered the great balancer, working along with the rest of the formula to help with stress, while having an anti-inflammatory action.

Suggested Dosage Echinacea 2-3 capsules, two to three times daily.

Ener-Jazz

Siberian Ginseng (GP .8% Total Eleuthrosides) *Eleuthrococcus senticosus*
Astragalus *Astragalus membranaceus*
American Ginseng *Panax quinquefolium*
Reishi *Ganoderma lucidum*
Licorice *Glycyrrhiza glabra*
Codonopsis *Codonopsis pilosula*
Polygonum *Polygonum cuspidatum*

This formula, with Siberian ginseng (GP .8% Total Eleuthrosides) as the major ingredient, has been used for stress (especially adrenal stress), energy, and to "chill" a person out, to be like a jazz musician. It has a combination of Oriental and Western herbs, in a very useful blend. Siberian ginseng (*Eleuthrococcus senticosus*) is a great energy herb, enlivening a person but calming them down at the same time. It doesn't have some of the overstimulating effects that can be found in Oriental ginsengs. This herb is a true adaptogen, helping a person respond better to a large range of stresses whether environmental, biological, personal and chemical.

Astragalus (*Astragalus membranaceus*) is a great tonic, especially for the immune system. American ginseng is similar to Oriental ginseng, but is gentler, like Siberian ginseng. Reishi (*Ganoderma lucidum*) is a very good calming herb, which also aids in nerve strength, insomnia and the immune system. Licorice, Codonopsis, and Polygonum help to balance out the formula.

Suggested Dosage 1/2-1 teaspoon, one to two times daily.

Essential Fatty Acids

There are several herbs that contain essential fatty acids. Four of the most commonly found herbs with essential fatty acids are Evening Primrose, Borage, Flax and Black Currant. The seed oils of these plants contain the omega-3 and omega-6 essential fatty acids. A mixture of these oils gives a full range of the essential fatty acids.

Lack of essential fatty acids can cause a large number of symptoms. Some of the most prominent symptoms of deficiency are: mood swings, abnormal clotting of blood platelets, heart attacks, stroke, high blood pressure, skin problems, eczema, hair loss, menstrual problems, fibrocystic breast disease, food allergies, ringing in the ears, migraine, decreased fertility, dry eyes, prostate enlargement and obesity.

Evening Primrose seed oil has had the most attention by the scientific community. It is high (7-10%) in gamma-linolenic acids (GLA) and other omega-6 series fatty acids. We require external sources of omega-3 and omega-6 essential fatty acids as the human body cannot manufacture them. Some of the body's uses of these oils involves a form that needs a set of enzymes (delta-6-desaturase) for conversion. GLA has already been converted and therefore doesn't require the presence of the enzyme.

Borage oil is similar to Evening Primrose oil in that it contains omega-6 series oils. It is noteworthy for its higher percentage of GLA (24%).

Flax seed oil has a large amount of essential fatty acid in both the omega-3 (linolenic) and omega-6 series (linoleic). Unfortunately, it has to be converted by essential, but often missing, enzymes to be able to produce many of the beneficial effects of fatty acids.

Black Currant Seed Oil also contains both omega-3 and omega-6 essential oils, with GLA (17%) already in the converted form.

A combination of the above oils satisfies the range of body needs for essential fatty acids.

Ester C

Ester C-500

Vitamin C (from Ester C)
500 mg
Calcium (from Ester C)
50 mg
Citrus Bioflavonoids
200 mg

Ester C-1000

Vitamin C (from Ester C)
1000 mg
Calcium (from Ester C)
100 mg
Citrus Bioflavonoids
200 mg

Ester C is a calcium ascorbate that contains naturally-occurring metabolites. This form of vitamin C has been found to be more absorbable, allowing the body to maintain higher body levels of Vitamin C for longer periods of time. Because of the neutralized pH, Ester C has been shown to be gentle and easier on the digestive tract than acid forms of Vitamin C.

Necessary for many of the body's cleansing processes, Vitamin C is recognized as an antioxidant, detoxifier and an essential nutrient for the formation and maintenance of connective tissue (teeth, gums, bone, muscle and cartilage). It is speculated that it is necessary for the release of folic acid from food and that it facilitates the absorption of iron.

The symptoms of Vitamin C deficiency are too numerous to list. Severe deficiency causes the medical condition known as scurvy. Some of the problems that arise if a person does not take enough Vitamin C are: frequent colds, fatigue, confusion, depression, bleeding gums, loose teeth, poor wound healing and back problems.

Citrus bioflavonoids have often been called Vitamin P or "permeability factors" because of their role in decreasing the "leakiness" and the fragility of capillaries. Many nutritionists think of this combination as a Vitamin C complex because they are all contained in foods high in C and seem to act in similar ways within the body.

Suggested Dosage 500 mg - 10,000 mg daily or as recommended by your health practitioner.

Fare You

(Chinese "vitamin U complex")

The root of the cabbage is high in S-methylmethionine, sometime called "vitamin U". It is not truly a vitamin, but has been shown to be effective in reducing ulcers. It stimulates the lining of the stomach to both prevent ulcers and to reverse ulcers if present. It works on gastric, duodenal or jejunal peptic ulcers quite well. It is fairly good for ulcers in the large intestinal tract. Results vary from 86 - 92% effectiveness in gastric ulcers. Clinically we hardly ever use anything else (though often adding Wei Te Ling) for ulcer complaints, because this formula works so well.

Ingredients Cabbage roots (high concentration of S-methylmethionine)

Suggested Dosage 2-4 tablets, with each meal or as directed.

Fargelin (high strength)

After many years of trying various formulas for patients with hemorrhoids, I discovered this wonderful Chinese formula. It is so much more effective than any other formula I have used, that it is rare for me to use anything else now. The fact that it is very economical is but a fortunate side benefit. Oral use of these pills is successful on both internal and external hemorrhoids and fissures, even if they are long standing. It is often combined with Fel Ursi ointment, which is used after bowel movements.

Succinum
Fel Ursi
Radix Pseudoginseng
Radix Scutellariae
Radix Corydalis
Radix Sanguisorbae
Flos sophorae
Callicarpa macrophylla

It is indicated for external and internal piles, prolapsus of the anus, and fresh blood after bowel evacuation.

Suggested Dosage 3 tablets, three times daily.

Fel Ursi Ointment

To sooth the burning and irritating feeling of hemorrhoids, this Chinese ointment has been quite successful. We normally use Fargelin (high strength) orally with this formula to reduce or reverse the hemorrhoids.

Musk
Mother of pearl
Zinkspath
Borneol
Yellowish Kaolin

Suggested Dosage apply externally after movements or two times daily.

Female Formula

Designed for women, this is used to correct hormonal imbalances such as those that occur at puberty, after pregnancy, menopause, upon the cessation of birth control pill usage or after a hysterectomy. This formula has also been found to be very useful for alleviating discomfort due to menstrual cramps, and reducing edema and depressions associated with the menstrual cycle. It may also strengthen the female organs.

Dong Quai (GP 1% Ferulic Acid) *Angelica sinensis*
Blue Cohosh *Caulophyllum thalictroides*
Black Cohosh *Cimicifuga racemosa*
Blessed Thistle *Centaurea benedicta*

Female Formula has also been used for hormonal irregularities in men, and is especially effective in the first stages of hormone-related balding.

Dong Quai (GP 1% Ferulic Acid), sometimes considered "female ginseng", has many positive effects on the female system. In the Orient, it is commonly used for menstrual irregularities, for menopause, for recuperating after childbirth and has been shown to be very helpful for women coming off hormone replacement therapy. Dong quai goes way beyond being a "female herb" though. It is quite appropriate for building up the system after being sick, fortifying the blood, and enhancing metabolism and oxygen utilization in the liver. Dong quai has also been shown to slow down male pattern baldness, to strengthen the heart, prevent atherosclerosis, prevent lipid deposits, function as an anti-bacterial agent, and work as a calming agent. Black Cohosh and Blue Cohosh help support the nervous and glandular system. Both of these (along with Blessed Thistle) are emmenagogues used both to build up and regulate the female reproductive system.

Suggested Dosage 2-3 capsules, two-three times daily.

Fertility Tea

I'm not even sure where the following tea formulas came from. I first noticed it in one of our student theses back in the late 70's. Since then I have used it with literally hundreds of couples with very good success. It has helped fertility in about 40-60% of people where nothing else works. Why the great variation between various years? I don't know. It is possibly the result of the varying quality of the constituent herbs bought in the local shops.

Suggested Dosage Both teas are simmered (one ounce in one quart of water) for ten minutes. Drink 1-3 cups daily for one - three months.

Female

Motherwort	3 parts
False Unicorn root	2 "
Licorice root	3 "
Wild Yam	2 "
Sarsaparilla	2 "
Marshmallow root	2 "
Ginseng	1 "
Uva Ursi	1 "
Ginger	1 "
Raspberry leaves	4 "
Ground Ivy	2 "

Male

Motherwort	2 "
False Unicorn root	1 "
Licorice root	3 "
Wild Yam	3 "
Sarsaparilla	3 "
Marshmallow root	3 "
Ginseng	1 "
Uva Ursi	2 "
Ginger	1 "
Raspberry leaves	4 "
Ground Ivy	2 "

Feverfew Plus Formula

Feverfew's (GP .5% Parthenolides) most notable feature is its outstanding ability to reduce the incidence of headaches and migraines. It has to build up in the system for 3-21 days before it works, but its action for most people is nothing short of miraculous. Feverfew acts by reducing platelet aggregation and by dilating the "micro vessels" in the head. Feverfew is also good as an anti-inflammatory, especially for arthritics. As its name implies, feverfew has often been used for colds and flus, especially if accompanied by a high temperature. There is great variability in the chemical constituents of this herb. Many commercial products have been tested and contain none of the active ingredients associated with migraine prophylaxis. This is a herb for which guaranteed potency (GP) is a must. Ginger root reduces platelet aggregation and is a blood stimulant. Willow bark aids in thinning blood and reducing platelet aggregation. Cayenne will lower cholesterol and reduce platelet aggregation.

Suggested Dosage 2 capsules, twice daily for one month. One capsule, twice daily in second month. Lower to one capsule daily by third month if headaches are stable.

Feverfew (GP .5% Parthenolides) *Tanacetum parthenium*
Ginger *Zingiber officinalis*
Willow bark *Salix sp.*
Cayenne *Capsicum ap.*

Four Ginsengs

These four plants come from the Ginseng botanical family (Araliaceae). Each herb has its own specific value, but all enhance body energies and are revered by local peoples as panaceas. Chinese ginseng increases energy. American ginseng aids in relaxing the body. Siberian ginseng helps people deal with stress, while Devil's Club helps control sugar and weight metabolism.

Suggested Dosage 1-2 capsules, twice daily.

Chinese Ginseng (GP 32% Ginsenosides) *Panax ginseng*
American Ginseng (GP 5% Ginsenosides) *Panax quinquefolium*
Siberian Ginseng (GP .8% Eleuthrosides) *Eleuthrococcus senticosus*
Devil's Club *Oplopanax horridum*

Ginkgo Plus Formula

Ginkgo *Ginkgo biloba* (50:1 GP 24% Flavoglycosides)
Gotu Kola *Centella asiatica*
Siberian Ginseng *Eleutrococcus senticosus*
Reishi *Ganoderma lucidum*
Ginger *Zingiber sp.*

There has been a lot of attention over the last several years paid to Ginkgo's (50:1 GP 24% Flavoglycosides) ability to increase memory. It is quite successful in this area. Not only does it increase blood circulation to the brain, it increases the amount of neural transmitters in the brain. It does this by both increasing the amount of neural transmitters emitted, and the number of receptor sites receiving the information. Ginkgo helps several other vascular circulation problems around the body, increasing microcirculation throughout the body. It also inhibits free radicals and platelet aggregation. Ginkgo has also been useful in the area of tinnitus (ringing in the ears), vertigo and hearing loss.

Gotu Kola has been used throughout Asia and in South America as a herb to increase longevity and to improve the memory. In folk medicine, a very long list of benefits are ascribed to it, often being considered to do almost everything. Siberian Ginseng is a good rejuvenating tonic and adaptogen, helping a person resist a large spectrum of stresses (physical, psychological, environmental, chemical and biological). Reishi can calm down the nervous system and aid in settling the mind. Sometimes memory is affected by the mind being too busy. Ginger is useful for aiding in circulation in general.

Suggested Dosage 2 capsules, twice daily.

Glucose Formula

Cedar berries *Juniperus monospermum*
Devil's Club *Oplapanax horridum*
Uva Ursi *Arctostaphylos uva-ursi*
Licorice root (GP 1% Glyerinic Acid) *Glycyrrhiza glabra*

Designed to enhance carbohydrate metabolism, Glucose Formula equalizes sugar levels in both high and low blood sugar conditions. It has also been found useful to help hypoglycemic individuals handle stress. This Glucose Formula also lowers one's craving for sugar. In addition to its sugar regulation function, it is formulated to strengthen the pancreas and adrenal glands while giving assistance to pancreatic digestive enzymes, making it a general pancreatic tonic.

Cedar Berry has been shown to be very successful in regulating insulin production, thus controlling sugar metabolism to a great extent. Devil's Club was once used officially as the medicine of choice for sugar metabolism problems such as diabetes. This herb also reduces cravings for sweets. Uva Ursi works as an effective diuretic and is used for adrenal support. Licorice root (GP 1% Glyerinic Acid) also gives adrenal support and aids in regulating blood sugar levels.

Suggested Dosage Two tablets, three times daily. In cases of diabetes this product should be used under the supervision of a qualified health practitioner.

Goldenseal Plus Formula

Goldenseal root extract (GP 10% Total Alkaloids) is considered the "King of the mucous membranes", and is specifically recommended for mucous membranes throughout the body, but especially the digestive, respiratory and urogenital tracts. The alkaloids in goldenseal are known to have a wide range of antibiotic action. Goldenseal has been shown to be specific for uterine contractions, excessive menstruation, and painful cycles. Goldenseal has become an endangered species in some parts of North America. All goldenseal used in a formula should ideally be cultivated for human use. Echinacea is known to be immuno-modulating, an antioxidant, to reduce wrinkling and have wound healing properties. Barberry and Gold Thread roots are antibiotic while strengthening the immune system. They also support mucous membrane integrity. Missouri Snake root has been mistaken for echinacea in research material but nonetheless has been shown to be immuno-modulating.

Goldenseal root extract (GP 10% Total Alkaloids) *Hydrastis canadensis*
Echinacea *Echinaceas sp.*
Barberry *Berberis vulgaris*
Gold Thread *Coptis chinensis*
Missouri Snake Root *Parthenium integrifolium*

Suggested Dosage 1-2 capsules, two to three times daily.

Note: Goldenseal should not be taken during pregnancy.

Hawthorn Plus Formula

Considered one of the great herbs for the heart muscle, hawthorn berry extract (GP 1.8% Vitexin) is useful for dilating coronary blood vessels, thereby delivering a more adequate blood supply to the organ. Studies have shown that hawthorn can increase the amount of oxygen going to the heart, increase enzyme metabolism in the heart muscle, act as a mild dilator of the heart muscle and reduce circulatory resistance through peripheral vasodilation. Hawthorn also has a mild diuretic action, useful for sore throats and strengthening to the kidneys. Hawthorn is heavily used in the Orient as a weight loss herb as it improves digestion, one of the common weight management problems. Cayenne is considered the great stimulant, used for blood circulation and as a heart tonic. Ginger is very good for circulation especially lowering peripheral resistance. Motherwort strengthens the heart and improves circulation.

Hawthorn berry extract (GP 1.8% Vitexin) *Crataegus oxycantha*
Cayenne seed pod (GP 90,000 Heat Units) *Capsicum sp.*
Ginger *Zingiber officinalis*
Motherwort *Leonurus cardiaca*

Suggested Dosage 2-3 capsules, two to three times daily.

Homeopathic Candida

Candida albicans 30X
Candida parapsilosis 30X
Pulsatilla 30X

This homeopathic formula has been extremely effective in eliminating yeast infection in the body. It works on a homeopathic principle called isonodes. This principle briefly states that by taking an organism that has become a problem, in homeopathic doses, you can eliminate it from the body. We have added *Candida parapsilosis* to the formula as it is the ancestor to *C. albicans*. Since there are so many "personal" strains of *C. albicans*, the addition of *C. parapsilosis* gives a deeper level of security for eradicating the yeast. *Pulsatilla* is used to treat several of the underlying symptoms related to the yeast condition.

Suggested Dosage 5-10 drops, three to four times daily (or as directed by health practitioner).

Inflammation Ointment

Cayenne pepper *Capsicum sp.*
Fireweed *Epilobium sp.*
Arnica *Arnica sp.*
Menthol

This formula is made in a liposome base, helping the absorption of the formula into the deeper tissue. It will help relax tissue, stop inflammation and relieve pain. Cayenne pepper (*Capsicum sp.*) contains a chemical called capsaicin, which has been shown to stop substance P, which is responsible for a wide variety of pain sensations. Fireweed (*Epilobium angustifolium*) can halt local inflammation by stopping the prostaglandin production responsible for the inflammation. Arnica (*Arnica montana*), used externally, has been very useful to move accumulated fluids in a local area, thus reducing congestion and therefore inflammation. Menthol (from mint leaves) gives a cooling, soothing aspect to the ointment.

Apply externally as needed

Kidney/Bladder Formula

Uva Ursi (GP 20% Hydroquinones as arbutin) *Arctostaphylos uva-ursi*
Juniper berries *Juniperus communis*
Buchu leaves *Barosma crenata*
Parsley leaves *Petroselinum sativum*
Marshmallow root *Althaea officinalis*
Ginger root *Zingiber officinalis*

Kidney/Bladder Formula is formulated to cleanse and build the renal (kidney/bladder) system. It has also been found useful for clearing congestion in the prostate gland.

Uva Ursi extract (GP 20% Hydroquinones as arbutin) contains a chemical called arbutin which changes into the urinary antiseptic hydroquinone in the kidneys, thus aiding to rid the urinary tract of infection. Uva Ursi is also an excellent diuretic, cleansing the kidneys and bladder, and is considered excellent in dissolving kidney sediment such as sand, gravel and even stones. Juniper berry is a urinary antiseptic as well as a diuretic. Buchu is specifically for the prostate and is an excellent diuretic. Parsley, a mild and soothing diuretic, is one of our most nutritious herbs, being exceptionally high in Vitamins A and C. Marshmallow is a very useful demulcent for the urinary tract, soothing the mucus membranes so as to avoid irritation from concentrated urine or calculi deposits. Ginger is used to stimulate peripheral circulation and to avoid griping in the urinary tract.

Suggested Dosage One or two capsules, two or three times a day.

Uva Ursi is most effective in an alkaline urine. It is suggested that an alkaline diet be followed when using this herbal formula.

Liver Formula

Milk Thistle extract (GP 80% Silymarin) *Silybum marianum*
Dandelion root *Taraxacum officinale*
Ginger root *Zingiber officinalis*
Burdock root *Arctium lappa*
Parsley root *Petroselinum sativum*
Black Radish *Raphanus sativus nigra*

Liver Formula is used to stimulate bile flow, decreasing cholesterol buildup in the gallbladder while dissolving calculi. This herbal formula can be used to detoxify the liver (hepatic) area, strengthen liver functions for blood cleansing and aid nutrient storage and many general hepatic functions.

Milk Thistle (GP 80% Silymarin) is considered the great liver herb. It has been shown to cleanse the liver, protect it from toxic substances, and aid in rebuilding it. It has been shown to be specific for rebuilding the liver from both cirrhosis (caused by alcohol toxicity), and hepatitis. Heavily used in European detox centers, it has had remarkable results for recuperating people who have eaten very poisonous mushrooms.

Black Radish can lower blood bilirubin levels through its cleansing action on the liver. Black Radish has also been shown to be the best herb for dealing with gallbladder congestion. Dandelion is one of the great herbs for the liver, both detoxifying and strengthen it. Dandelion also aids in cleaning the blood and has immuno-modulating properties. Ginger is beneficial for the circulation in the liver as well as supporting the tubular functions in the liver/gallbladder area. The anti-microbial action of ginger, along with its soothing action on the entire digestive system helps enhance this formula.

Burdock is quite strengthening to the liver, with detoxifying and immuno-modulating properties. Parsley root and dandelion roots are both known for their hepatic qualities and for their ability to dissolve gallstones or prevent formation.

Suggested Dosage One to two capsules, two to four times daily.

Lower Bowel Tonic

Cascara sagrada extract (GP 20-30% Hydroxyanthracene derivatives) *Rhamnus purshiana*
Buckthorn *Rhamnus catharticus*
Ginger *Zingiber sp.*
Goldenseal root *Hydastis canadensis*
Raspberry leaves *Rubus idaeus*
Fennel seed *Anethum foeniculum*
Turkey rhubarb *Rheum palmatum*
Lobelia *Lobelia inflata*
Cayenne pepper *Capsicum minimum*

Lower Bowel Tonic comes from a generic group of herbal formulas that are specific for the colon and benefit the digestive tract. The **exact** ratio of herbs has great significance on how well it works.

Although it has a cleansing or laxative effect, its major functions are to increase muscle tone and flexibility of the intestinal wall and to correct neural and hormonal control throughout the system. Many practitioners of natural methods strongly believe that a clean and healthy colon is the first and perhaps the most important step toward better health. The problem is that many "laxative type" formulas are "addictive" in the sense that the longer you take them, the more you need to take to get the same action. This formula is quite different. Working on muscle tone, it strengthens the colon, instead of just causing bowel movement. After taking this formula for several months the patient needs less for the same action.

Cascara Sagrada (GP 20-30% Hydroxyanthracene derivatives), buckthorn and Turkey Rhubarb are the major components. All have a group of glycosides in them that stimulate catharsis. Two of these glycosides, emodin and chrysophanic acid, work similarly to the brakes and gas pedal in a car, controlling the motility of the colon. This control causes the major building feature of this formula. Cascara Sagrada not only acts as a laxative but restores natural tone to the colon.

Ginger and fennel seeds help reduce griping or nausea in the intestinal tract during the cleansing phase. Goldenseal strengthens the mucous membranes while raspberry leaves work as a demulcent, soothing the intestinal tract. Lobelia works on nervous control and the cayenne increases the blood circulation.

Suggested Dosage 2-3 capsules, two-three times daily or as needed. Diarrhea is often experienced for the first few days. If this continues after the third day, decrease dose accordingly.

Lung Formula

This herbal formula is specific for dilating bronchial tubes while cleansing mucus from the bronchioles, lungs and sinuses. It has been found useful for airborne allergies, sinus congestion and lung problems.

Ma Huang (GP 5% Alkaloids), the major ingredient of this herbal formula, has been one of the most important herbs of Chinese medicine for over 5,000 years. Its major chemical, ephedrine, used extensively in Western medicine since 1923, works on the autonomic nervous system to cause dilation of the bronchial tubes and alveoli. It has also been shown to be a great cleanser of the respiratory mucous membranes.

Mullein leaves (demulcent, expectorant and diuretic), and coltsfoot leaves (expectorant, demulcent and diuretic) are both specific for the respiratory system. Goldenseal, the "King of the mucous membranes", improves membrane quality, while regulating the quantity of mucus in the respiratory system. Lobelia herb works on the nerve supply to the lungs and is also an excellent expectorant. Cayenne stimulates blood circulation, aiding in the supply of nutrients.

Suggested Dosage One to three capsules, two to three times daily.

Should be used only under the supervision of a qualified health practitioner in cases of high blood pressure or heart disease.

Ma Huang extract (GP 5% Alkaloids) *Ephedra sinica*
Mullein leaf *Verbascum thapsus*
Goldenseal *Hydrastis canadensis*
Coltsfoot *Tussilago farfara*
Marshmallow *Althaea officinalis*
Lobelia herb *Lobelia inflata*
Cayenne *Capsicum minimum*

Men's Formula

Saw Palmetto Extract (GP 25% Fatty Acids) is famous for its action on the prostate. It can be quite effective in altering the biochemical process that triggers enlargement of the prostate called benign prostatic hyperplasia (BPH) in men. There have been more than 20 studies showing that saw palmetto can have a dramatic action in as little as 30 days. Saw palmetto has also been shown to have an immune-stimulating effect, act as a mild diuretic and may increase breast size in developing girls. The active ingredient in this herb needs to be extracted in a specific way to ensure it effectiveness.

Saw Palmetto extract (GP 25% Fatty acids) *Serenoa ripens*
Buchu *Barosma betulina*
Uva Ursi *Arctostaphylos uva-ursi*
Corn Silk *Zea mays*
Zinc

Buchu is a prostate tonic blood cleanser and mild diuretic. Uva Ursi is one of the great diuretics with an antibiotic effect on the urogenital system. Corn silk is soothing to the urogenital system with a mild diuretic property. Zinc is a mineral supplement that supports the prostate.

Suggested Dosage 2-3 capsules, two to three times daily.

Multiminerals (Krebs Cycle)

Calcium	500 mg
Magnesium	200 mg
Potassium	99 mg
Zinc	30 mg
Copper	2 mg
Manganese	10 mg
Selenium	200 mcg
Molybdenum	50 mcg
Iodine	150 mcg
Chromium	200 mcg
Boron	200 mcg
Vanadium	50 mcg

In a fruit base of extracts of Rose Hip, Cranberry, Raspberry, Grapeskin and Pineapple.

A multimineral based on the Krebs cycle concept with the minerals coming from acid bases (eg. calcium citrate) helps in the absorption of the minerals. The fruit base provides other "mystery" substances that will help in absorption and utilization.

Suggested Dosage 2 tablets, twice daily or as directed by health practitioner.

Multivitamins and minerals

Four tablets contain

Beta-carotene	10,000 IU
Vitamin A	5,000 IU
Ester C	250 mg
Thiamine (B_1)	30 mg
Riboflavin (B_2)	50 mg
Niacin (B_3)	50 mg
Pyridoxine (B_6)	50 mg
Vitamin B_{12}	50 mcg
Biotin	300 mcg
Folic acid	400 mcg
Pantothenic acid	50 mg
PABA	50 mg
Choline	50 mg
Inositol	50 mg
Vitamin D	400 IU
Vitamin E	400 IU
Calcium Citrate	1,000 mg
Iron	18mg
Iodine (Kelp)	150 mcg
Magnesium Citrate	400 mg
Zinc chelate	25 mg
Copper chelate	2 mg
Potassium	90 mg
Manganese	2 mg
Chromium chelate	200 mcg
Boron	200 mcg
Selenium	50 mcg
Molybdenum	50 mcg
GP flavonoids	100 mg
Hesperidin	25 mg
Rutin	25 mg
Octacosanol	250 mcg

In choosing a product which contains all of the vitamins and essential minerals, ideally it will contain many of the additional supplements used throughout the text. This formula can often suffice for many of the nutrients we talk about under the various health conditions.

Suggested Dosage Take two tablets, twice daily or four tablets throughout the day.

Muscle Relaxing Formula

Kava Kava root extract (GP 30% Kavalactones) *Piper methysticum*
Valerian Root *Valeriana officinalis*
Hops *Humulus lupulus*
Skullcap *Scutellaria lateriflora*
Catnip *Nepata cataria*
Lemon balm *Melissa officinalis*

The key ingredient in this formula is Kava Kava root (GP 30% Kavalactones), the most powerful herbal muscle relaxant known. Working on the motor units (the point of muscle-nerve coordination), Kava Kava increases general flexibility, aiding in soft tissue tension and helping in structural adjustment. This muscle relaxant herb helps to reduce the effect of stress on the body. Besides working on the muscles, it has a distinct relaxing effect on the digestive and urinary tract. This herb not only supports relaxation in the body, it enhances mental clarity. Valerian root is a relaxant, helpful in alleviating insomnia, lowering blood pressure and stress on the heart. Hops has a sedative property that aids in relaxation and sleep. Skullcap relaxes the mind, while having antispasmodic and anti-inflammatory properties. Catnip is known to relax the body, reducing headaches and calming the digestive tract. Lemon balm, a little used but an important herb is calming to the system, especially the digestive tract.

Suggested Dosage Two-three capsules, three times daily, increase as needed.

Nerve Formula

Valerian extract (GP .8% Valerenic acids) (4:1) *Valeriana officinalis*
Oats *Avena sp.*
Hops *Humulus lupulus*
Skullcap *Scutellaria lateriflora*
Kava Kava *Piper methysticum*
Passionflower *Passiflora spp.*

Individuals vary in their ability to cope with circumstances and surroundings. Nervousness could be described as a state of mental and/or physical restlessness.

Symptoms include a person who is fidgety, easily startled, sleepless, restless, anxious or fatigued. A feeling of unpleasantness or sometimes even of fright can occur making concentration difficult or impossible.

Valerian (GP .8% Valerenic acids) yields isovalerianic acid giving a soothing, calming and sedative effect. Oats and passionflower have been shown to be tonics and relaxants to the nervous system. Skullcap yields scutellarin. Hops yields lupulinic acid and humulon, all giving a soothing and calming effect.

Suggested Dosage One - three capsules before meals and one-three at bedtime, daily.

Parasite Formula

Sweet Annie *Artemisia annua*
Black Walnut Hulls *Juglans niger*
Grapefruit seed extract *Citrus X parodisi*

The occurence of parasites in the body is much more common than most people think. These can range from small pin worms to hock worms, liver flukes and tape worms. This simple parasite formula is designed to take care of all varieties. We can also have invaders, such as fungi (*Candida albicans*) etc. Many of these organisms will at least be inhibited from growing when using this formula. There is a recent resurgence of an old theory that many of our most critical health issues stems from internal parasites. Some people feel that many types of cancer might have their start with parasites. We can say that parasites will at least weaken the body, and most likely the immune system with their presence.

The major herb in this formula is *Artemisia annua* (Sweet Annie). It has had quite a bit of research around it in the last several years. It has been used in the Orient for a long time as an excellent parasite herb. Present studies show that it is one of the most potent cures for malaria, both as a preventive and after getting bitten by malarial insects. It is recommended when going on an adventure that takes one into the tropics. The Chinese use it "to resolve summer heat". It makes handling hot weather much easier.

Black Walnut (green hulls) are one of the well-established parasite herbs from the West. It has been used for centuries for intestinal parasites. Grapefruit seed extract is very good at lowering the incidence of microorganism problems.

Suggested Dosage 2 capsules, twice daily for one month, take a month break and consume acidophilus-like bacteria for one month. Repeat 2 - 4 times.

Phoenix Formula

Wuchi Paifeng Wan or Women's Tea

This traditional Chinese formula has been used for female complaints for centuries. It is used to tone up the female organs, help alleviate infertility and regulate menstrual flow. It is a very complex formula with a special type of black meat chicken as the major ingredient.

Suggested Dosage After menstrual flow, take one "egg", open, split contents into three equal sized parts. Take one part, three times a day, consuming one egg's worth daily. Repeat this for ten days and stop. After the next menstrual flow, repeat the whole process. This is usually done for three - six months.

Gallus Domesticus
Radix Ginseng
Colla Cornus Cervi
Radix Astragali Seu Hedysari
Radix Angelicae sinsensis
Radix Paeoniae alba
Radix Rehmanniae
Rehmanniae praeparatae
Rhizoma Dioscoreae
Rhizoma Cyperi
Carapax Trionycis
Concha Ostreae
O'otheca Mantidis
Radix Salviae miltiorrhizae
Rhizoma Ligustici chuanxiong
Radix Asparagi
Radix Stellariae
Semen Euryales
Coru Cervir degelatinatum
Radix Glycyrrhizae

Psyllax

This formula is a bulk laxative and hydrophilic bulking agent that soothes the intestinal tract. It is specific for colon irritations, ulcerations and spasms. As a bulking agent it has functioned to suppress appetite while cleansing the intestinal tract, making it very useful for weight control programs. It is also an effective astringent in firming up diarrhea. The major factor in determining if it is used as a laxative or an astringent is the amount of liquid taken during the day. Taking less than 3-4 cups of liquid will give Psyllax a firming action. More than 7 cups gives it a laxative action.

Psyllium husk, the major component of this formula causes the bulking action in a mucillagenous base. Comfrey, whey powder, marshmallow and Slippery Elm all work on the quantity and quality of mucus in the intestinal tract. Echinacea , Shepherd's Purse, bayberry and bentonite all aid in detoxification. Wild yam works on spasms and cramping in the intestinal tract. Kelp helps regulate mineral balance.

Suggested Dosage One tablespoon in a glass of water or juice (tastes best in tomato or apple) morning and evening, or as directed by a practitioner.

Psyllium Husk *Plantago psyllium*
Comfrey *Symphytum officinale*
Whey powder
Marshmallow root *Althaea officinalis*
Slippery Elm bark *Ulmus fulva*
Echinacea *Echinacea angustifolia*
Powdered Bentonite
Shepherd's Purse *Capsella bursa-pastoris*
Wild Yam *Dioscorea sp.*
Kelp *Fucus versiculosus*
Bayberry bark *Myrica cerifera*

Reishi Plus Formula

Reishi extract (GP 14% Triterpenes) 15:1 *Ganoderma lucidum*
Echinacea purpurea
Echinacea angustifolia
Ginger Root *Zingiber officinalis*
Barberry *Berberis vulgaris*

Reishi (GP 14% Triterpenes) has become a central product in my clinical practice. In a sentence, it will calm a person down. There is a formula in China that translates into English ... "to protect an academic from their own brain." This calming effect is one of Reishi's best attributes. It has also been very good for treating digestive problems, asthma, allergies, insomnia, as an immune tonic, CFS, fibromyalgia, AIDS, sugar metabolism problems and even cancer.

Both of the Echinaceas are known as immune modulators, by strengthening and regulating the immune system. Ginger is a great stimulant, specific for the digestive tract and lungs. Barberry is a good herbal antibiotic and tonic, toning up the mucous membranes of the body.

Suggested Dosage 2-3 capsules, two - three times daily.

SAF for Kids

Each six capsules contain

Vitamin C (from Ester C)	60 mg
Calcium	100 mg
Vitamin B_6	50 mg
Magnesium	50 mg
GABA	800 mg
Passionflower Extract(6:1)	500 mg
L-Taurine	500 mg

SAF for Kids was designed specifically for kids as a stress and anxiety formula. Its major use is for children who are hyperactive or have attention deficit disorder. It is a blend of vitamins, minerals, amino acids and passionflower.

Suggested Dosage 2 - 6 capsules per day

Shih Chuan Ta Pu Wan

Codonopsis pilosula
Ligusticum wallichii
Astragalus membranaceus
Glycyrrhiza uralensis
Paeonia albiflora (white)
Atractylodes macrocephala
Poria cocos
Rhemannia glutinosa (processed)
Angelica sinensis
Cinnamomum cassia

This Chinese energy/stress tonic is one of the best little formulas I have ever found for the busy worker. This traditional patent medicine is a very economical way to give a person a lift. It works on building the entire endocrine system, while calming a person down. It is especially beneficial as a mid-afternoon pick-me-up, when one is overly stressed and worn out.

Suggested Dosage 8 tablets; three times daily. We suggest between 4 - 15 tablets, one - four times daily.

Sleeping Formula

Melatonin
Hops *Humulus lupulus*
Chamomile *Chamomilla nobilis*
Passionflower *Passiflora sp.*
Oatstraw *Avena sp.*

This formula comes in a capsule form and is a very good herbal relaxant, pain reliever and sleeping tablet. Melatonin is well known for its ability to help a person fall asleep. It is specific for co-ordinating circadian rhythms and can thereby reduce jet lag. Hops is one of the more famous sleeping herbs, both relaxing the mind and calming the body. Chamomile has a gentle, calming effect while passionflower and oatstraw strengthen the nervous system.

Suggested Dosage For sleeping, 1-3 tablets a half hour before bed.

St. John's Wort Extract Plus Formula

St. John's Wort extract (GP .3% Hypericin) *Hypericum perforatum*
Reishi mushroom *Ganoderma lucidum*
Wild Oats *Avena sativa*
Lavender Flower *Lavandula angustifolia*
Sweet Annie *Artemisia annua*

St. John's Wort (GP .3% Hypericin) has become quite popular because of its strong antiviral and antibacterial action. This has made it quite effective in treatment programs established for Chronic Fatigue Syndrome, herpes, hepatitis and even HIV. An additional, and very important, effect of St. John's Wort is its antidepressant properties. This is particularly useful as many people with viral problems also display symptoms of depression or suffer from nervousness. The active constituent in St. John's Wort responsible for this antidepressant effect is hypericin, which has been shown to reduce both emotional and physical stress. Tissue under stress also receives an increased blood supply during consumption of this herb. St. John's Wort is also known to be a uterine tonic, has a strengthening effect on the heart, aorta, arterioles, lungs and bladder. It can be used for dysentery, worms and has even shown some promise in U.S. National Cancer Institute initial studies on tumor systems.

Reishi mushroom is put in this formula for both its ability to calm the mind and to strengthen the immune system. Wild Oats will strengthen and calm the nerves, working as a nerve tonic. Lavender flowers are soothing for emotions and nerves. Sweet Annie has antibacterial and antiviral properties.

Suggested Dosage 1-3 capsules, two to three times daily.

Stomach Formula

Meadowsweet *Spirea ulmaria*
Gentian *Gentiana lutea*
Goldenseal *Hydrastis canadensis*
Fennel Seed *Anethum foeniculum*
Fenugreek Seed *Trigonella foenum-graecum*
Lobelia *Lobelia inflata*

Stomach Formula is designed to work as a general tonic for the stomach and digestive system with its major purpose to stimulate the production of hydrochloric acid (HCl). By stimulating other digestive enzymes from the pancreas and liver, the formula offers an advantage to a large proportion of North American society who do not digest food properly. Many herbal practitioners use this formula at the beginning of any rebuilding program when lack of proper digestion is a factor in the overall condition of the patient.

Meadowsweet is the major herb, shown to regulate gastric secretion, increasing HCl in hypoacidic conditions and decreasing it in hyperacidic conditions of the stomach. Goldenseal, "King of the mucous membranes", acts specifically as a tonic to the digestive system. Gentian is one of the classic bitter herbs used to increase appetite and to enhance digestion. Fennel and fenugreek both work as cleansing agents, working on excessive mucus in the digestive tract and as digestive tonics. Fennel also acts as a carminative, reducing griping of the intestines and relieving indigestion. Fenugreek is a demulcent and is soothing for inflamed conditions of the stomach. Cayenne increases the circulation to the parietal cells of the stomach thus ensuring that the proper nutrients are present for the manufacture of HCl. Lobelia aids in both autonomic nerve and hormone control to coordinate and regulate the digestive functions. This formula, instead of giving the body digestive enzymes as an outside aid, stimulates the body to produce its own.

Suggested Dosage One to two capsules with the two major meals of the day.

Note: If a person has a large accumulation of mucus in the digestive tract, some nausea may be experienced during the first few days of use. This happens with less than 10% of users and may be avoided by taking the supplement in the middle of the meal.

Tan Kwe Gin

This tonic, usually reserved for females, is often given to a woman after delivering a child. It is designed to nourish the blood and sooth menses. It can also be used as a general tonic, fortifying muscle and blood. It is indicated in weakness, pale complexion, anemia, headache, dizziness and for convalescence. It can also be used by men as a tonic.

Suggested Dosage 1-2 tablespoons, two times daily, usually for two months.

Radix Angelicae sinensis
Coila Corii asnii
Radix Codonopsis
Radix Astragalus
Radix Paeonia alba
Poria cocos
Rhizome Chunxiong
Radix Glycyrhhizae
Sugar

Trauma Ointment

This homeopathic ointment's effectiveness is close to magical. I have used it for years on all kinds of injuries, athletic or accidental. It was designed for any kind of trauma such as sprained ankles, torn ligaments, burns and bruises. It also can be used for acne, arthritis and wounds.

Apply the ointment generously over the area 2-6 times daily.

Arnica montana
Calendula officinalis
Echinacea angustifolia
Hamamella virginiana
Echinacea purpurea
Chamomilla sp.
Symphytum officinalis
Bellis perennis
Hypericum perforatum
Millefollium
Aconitum nap 1X
Belladonna 1X
Mercurius solub Hah 6X
Hepar sulphuris cal 6X

Vaginal Suppository

This product is the Homeopathic Candida formula made into a suppository. Use one daily for six days, stop one day and douche with equal parts apple cider vinegar and water and insert an acidophilus capsule. Repeat at least once.

Valerian Plus Formula

Valerian (GP 1% Valerenic acid) is a great relaxant for the nervous system. It can aid in reducing stress by day and alleviate insomnia by night. Valerian can also lower blood pressure, quiet a stressed heart, be antibacterial and strengthen the liver. Kava Kava root is a very good muscle relaxant that calms down the mind, and the urinary and digestive tract. Hops is a sedative that can aid in relaxation and sleep. Skullcap can relax the mind, and be an antispasmodic with anti-inflammatory properties. Catnip will relax the body, reduce headaches, and calm the digestive tract. Lemon balm is calming to the system, especially the digestive tract.

Valerian root extract (GP 1% Valerenic acid) *Valeriania officinalis*
Kava Kava *Piper methysticum*
Hops *Humulus lupulus*
Skullcap *Scutellaria lateriflora*
Lemon Balm *Melissa officinalis*

Suggested Dosage 1-2 capsules, twice daily and 2 capsules before bed.

Vegetable Silica Formula

Oat Straw *Avena sativa*
Horsetail *Equisetum spp.*
Borage *Borago officinalis*
Nettles *Urtica dioica*

Vegetable silica is a traditional formula that is quite high in silica. Silica is necessary for building the hair and nails. There are many practitioners in holistic practice who believe in a concept of biological transmutations put forward by Louis Kervran. If this concept is true, it is suggested that silica will increase the amount of calcium in the body. A similar formula has been used in the health food industry for years as a herbal source of calcium.

Suggested Dosage 2 capsules, twice daily.

Wei Te Ling

Os Sepiae
Rhizoma Corydalis
Honey

This Chinese patent medicine is very good for relaxing tension in the stomach or intestinal tract. It is indicated for an overactive stomach, poor digestion, ulcers, indigestion and gas.

Suggested Dosage 4-6 tablets, three times daily taken with hot water.

White Flower Embrocation

Pak Fah Yeow

Menthol Crystal
Wintergreen Oil
Eucalyptus Oil
Camphor
Lavender Oil

This traditional Chinese formula has been used for all kinds of household complaints. It is used for muscle cramps, menstrual cramps, headaches, nausea, digestive problems, laryngitis, colds and flus. The combination of these volatile oils can lift one's spirit and be quite antibiotic in nature. It can be added to a humidifier to help with asthma, coughs, colds and flu.

Suggested Dosage 1-5 drops. Rub onto sore area or rub on hand and inhale.

Encyclopedia of Ailments and Treatments

Abscess

An abscess may occur anywhere in the body and is a condition indicating local infection. White blood cells, known as leukocytes, collect in pockets in the infected area together with dead tissue cells and other substances to form pus - a dense opaque fluid. The function of the white blood cells is to fight infection and assist in rebuilding damaged tissue.

Recommended Action

A good drawing poultice can be made up of a combination of the "single herbs". This should be spread thickly over the entire area to bring the abscess to a head. Hot onions or fresh ground garlic (applied after a coating of olive oil), hot pumpkin or hot uncooked tomatoes can be used in lieu of the suggested herbs if they are unavailable. After expansion, bursting and drainage is complete, a good healing and tissue building poultice should be applied. The herbs may also be taken internally to speed healing, and at the same time a ten-day Cleansing Diet (see Appendix) should be implemented. Removing mucus-forming foods (see Mucus) from the diet and thoroughly cleansing the blood should prevent a recurrence of the condition.

Single Herbs Plantain (drawing); Comfrey (heals and rebuilds tissue); Garlic (disinfectant and tissue builder, apply a layer of olive oil first to prevent blistering); Chaparral, Burdock root or Echinacea (blood cleansers); Goldenseal root (disinfectant), Slippery Elm bark (soother and builder).

Combinations A good drawing poultice can be made from 3 parts Goldenseal root, 1 part Myrrh, 2 parts Slippery Elm bark, 3 parts Plantain, and 1 part Comfrey.

This poultice should be alternated with the fresh ground garlic poultice mentioned above. For the necessary internal cleansing, take two Goldenseal Plus Formula and two capsules of Cleansing Formula, twice daily after meals. The bowel must be kept clean through use of Lower Bowel Tonic if necessary.

Synergistic Vitamins and Minerals Beta-CEZB$_6$, Vitamin C (500 mg, three to six times daily); Vitamin A (10,000 IU), Zinc (15 mg, two times daily). Apply Vitamin E oil after abscess is drained.

Acne Case

One of the most important things to remember about acne problems is the psychological implication that often surrounds it. Once people, especially during puberty, see acne they get upset about their appearance and often the emotional response makes the acne worse. Fortunately, seeing an improvement often has the same effect. They see that they are getting better and by feeling better about themselves emotionally, they often improve faster. The most important thing to consider is to start the process in a positive direction.

Acne

Acne, a chronic disorder of the sebaceous glands which produces oily substances on the skin, occurs most commonly during puberty and adolescence. At this time, sex-related hormones are especially active and affect the secretions of the sebaceous glands. Hormonal imbalance can often be caused by emotional stress resulting in excessive oil secretion. When the system attempts to excrete toxins through the skin, it causes the oil to become dry and hard, thus clogging the pores, producing swelling, soreness and redness. A common modern diet high in meat, deep fried foods, concentrated starches and sugars loads the system with toxic waste. This diet also lacks the necessary nutrients for maintenance of an adequate hormone balance. Often the emotional response to one's appearance, especially during puberty, makes the acne worse. Bacterial infections are often associated with acne and are the direct result of picking or squeezing which irritates the skin eruptions.

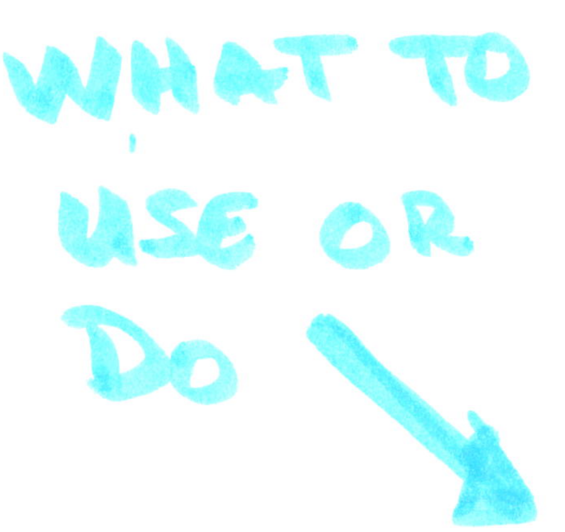

Recommended Action

A change of diet is very important, starting with a D-tox Diet or a 7-10 day Cleansing Diet (see Appendix) to eliminate toxic wastes in the blood and bowels. Avoid strong acidic foods such as meats, sugars and refined starches. Whole grains help to correct hormonal imbalances and therefore should be included in the diet after the Cleansing Diet. They are especially useful if sprouted or soaked overnight to change their pH. Millet, buckwheat and brown rice already have a suitable pH.

Single Herbs Burdock root, Dandelion root, Echinacea or Sassafras (blood cleansers); Kelp, Alfalfa and Dandelion root (vitamins & minerals); Buckthorn, Turkey Rhubarb, Cascara Sagrada (bowel cleansers); Liquid Chlorophyll, Siberian Ginseng, Aloe Vera.

Combinations Lower Bowel Tonic, Cleansing Formula. If hormone imbalance is suspected (as in puberty or after childbirth), use Female Formula for both males and females. If liver problems are suspected, use the Liver Formula.

Synergistic Vitamins and Minerals Beta-CEZB_6, Vitamin A, B complex, Vitamin C, Calcium, Magnesium, Zinc, Vitamin E, and Multivitamins and minerals.

Suggested Program

Start with a 12 day D-tox Diet or 7 to 10 day Cleansing Diet, then adopt a maintenance diet. It should be noted that the acne often gets worse before it get better during the cleansing phase.

Breakfast two Beta-CEZB_6, three Female Formula, Trauma Ointment in morning.

Morning Snack Ester C (500 mg).

Lunch 1/4 cup Aloe Vera juice or gel. It can be switched to another time in day if needed.

Afternoon Snack Ester C (500 mg).

Supper Same supplements as breakfast.

Evening B complex with 125 mg Niacin.

AIDS (Acquired Immune Deficiency Syndrome)

AIDS is a serious disease that is characterized by the body's inability to defend itself. The onset may be sudden or gradual. No one dies of AIDS. Other opportunistic infections and diseases overtake the body due to the crippled immune system. One part of the immune system is represented by the T-lymphocyte cells (white blood cells). Two of the types of T-lymphocytes are "T-helper" and "T-suppressor". AIDS occurs when there is a decrease in the ratio of T-helper to T-suppressor cells. With a small number of helper cells the body is almost defenseless against many opportunistic diseases. Usually the person dies of an overwhelming amount of infection and/or cancer. The most common death is due to pneumonia and Kaposi's sarcoma (a connective tissue cancer). Some of the other most common infections are cytomegalovirus (CMV), Epstein-Barr virus (EBV), Herpes simplex virus (HSV), tuberculosis (TB) or Candida. The majority of scientific thinkers feel that AIDS is caused by Human Immunodeficiency virus (HIV).

At the first stages of HIV infection, most people are unaware they are carriers. It has been shown the HIV can be transmitted by sexual contact, through intravenous drug use, blood transfusions, and during pregnancy to the fetus. Condoms and spermicides are considered 90% effective against the transmission of the HIV virus. It is estimated that about 20-38% of HIV-positive people develop full fledged AIDS within five years.

Recommended Action

There is no known cure for AIDS. The most important approach is to keep the immune system constantly alert and reduce as many factors as possible that can suppress the immune system. Many HIV-positive people are living satisifying healthy lives by following a few simple rules for strengthening the immune system. A person that has a lifestyle contributing to risk factors or a person that is HIV-positive has to be more careful than the average person. The diet should be simple with as few refined foods as possible. Sugar, dairy, flour, preservatives and other additives seem to be particularly bad. Poor digestion and malabsorption can also be contributing factors, especially poor assimilation of minerals like zinc. We therefore often suggest digestive enzymes, watching for irritable bowel syndrome, diarrhea and constipation.

It is very common for a person with AIDS to also have a Candida infection. The Candida diet is a good diet to follow for this group of people. Stress is a big factor. Many types of stress can contribute to increased probability of forming AIDS. Social disapproval, loss of a loved one due to AIDS, loneliness, guilt and isolation have all been shown to contribute to loss of self-esteem. These emotional factors seem to weaken the immune system, contributing to the speed at which a person can succumb to AIDS and even death. Positive emotions can be the single strongest contributing factor to increasing the immune function. There have been studies that show a person can increase immune function by simply watching a funny video.

Other things that should be considered are: stopping smoking, getting adequate sleep, having some creative outlets, and getting fresh air and clean food. The diet should have adequate beta-carotene, B vitamins, zinc, iron, essential amino acids. On the other hand, excessive amounts of cholesterol, Vitamin E (more than 600 IU/day), zinc (more than 100 mg daily), and polyunsaturated fatty acids can weaken the immune system. It appears that a healthy lifestyle and optimal nutrition can extend a person's life and help in the quality of life for many HIV-positive and AIDS patients.

Single Herbs Reishi, Cat's Claw, Astragalus, Echinacea, Goldenseal, other mushrooms (enoke, shiitake, maitake), Pau d'arco, Licorice, Lomatia, Osha, Garlic. There is some controversy over the use of Echinacea though we've had very good clinical success with it among HIV-positive patients for more than 10 years.

Combinations Reishi Plus Formula, Goldenseal Plus Formula, Echinacea Plus Formula.

Attitude and AIDS

Probably one of the most significant factors to keep the immune system functioning properly is emotional attitude. One person doing active research in this area is Louise Hayes. She has had a very good success rate with AIDS patients. She has shown, on a practical level, that a positive attitude, with self-respect, can be very beneficial to the health of AIDS patients. Obtaining one of her books on the subject might prove useful. There has been an increasing amount of research in this area by others. A good laugh has been shown to boost the amount of immune lymphocyte action. I have seen a big difference in the long term health of patients with AIDS who have created a positive environment for themselves. T-helper cells are not the only means of turning on the function of the immune system.

Synergistic Vitamins and Minerals Beta-CEZB$_6$ (two tablets, twice daily), Beta-carotene (50,000 IU, twice daily), B complex, Vitamin C (minimum 5 grams daily), bioflavonoids, Zinc (up to 60 mg daily), copper (3 mg daily).

Suggested Program

Breakfast Reishi extract (3 capsules), Echinacea Plus Formula (2 capsules), Beta-CEZB$_6$ (2 tablets), Chlorella (5-10 tablets), Beta-carotene (30,000 IU), Cat's Claw (2-6 capsules)
Morning snack Ester C (1,000-2,000 mg)
Lunch Reishi extract (2 capsules), Aloe Vera (1/2 cup)
Afternoon snack Ester C (1,000-2,000 mg)
Supper same as breakfast
Evening snack Ester C (1,000-2,000 mg)

Afterbirth pains

These spasmodic pains occur immediately after childbirth and during the next few days. Uterine contractions are experienced the strongest while nursing the baby. Their function is to prevent hemorrhage by constricting the capillaries in the uterine wall where the placenta was recently attached. The cramps serve a necessary and useful purpose, but may sometimes cause severe discomfort.

Single Herbs Fennel (antispasmodic); St. John's Wort (astringent and sedative); Cramp Bark (antispasmodic); Dong Quai, Siberian Ginseng.

Combinations Female Formula (aids in adjusting hormones), TanKwe Gin, Nerve Formula. If colon is not active, use Lower Bowel Tonic.

Synergistic Vitamins and Minerals Vitamin E, B complex, Magnesium Phosphate (6X) tissue salt, Calcium/Magnesium.

Suggested Program

Two Female Formula, three times daily, TanKwe Gin (one tablespoon, two times daily for two bottles), Calcium (600 mg), Magnesium (300 mg), Magnesium Phosphate 6X-12X tissue salt (10 drops, four to six times daily), Lower Bowel Tonic as needed.

Ague

Ague (recurrent spasmodic shaking) is commonly associated with malarial fevers. Unlike other fits of shivering, this condition often continues after normal body temperature has been restored. As the condition progresses, feverish spells alternate with chills. The body attempts to warm itself by spontaneous contraction of the involuntary muscles. Malaria, pneumonia and some other fever-producing maladies can be accompanied by or preceded by ague.

Recommended Action

The best treatment is to encourage the fever with diaphoretic herbs and plenty of moist heat until it breaks, unless it approaches dangerously high levels. In this case, febrifuge herbs should be employed to reduce the fever (see Fevers).

Single Herbs Thyme or Hops (febrifuges); Bayberry, Blessed Thistle, Catnip, Tame Sage, Chamomile, Yarrow (diaphoretics).

Synergistic Vitamins and Minerals B complex, Vitamin C, Calcium, Magnesium Phosphate (6X) tissue salt.

Allergies

Hayfever, asthma, hives, nausea, dizziness, diarrhea, headaches, chills and inflammation of the skin are common allergic reactions. Allergens create these conditions in persons who are hyper(over) sensitive to them. In an effort to rid itself of the obnoxious substance, the body overreacts to the presence of the allergen and produces large quantities of antibodies and excessive amounts of histamine.

Recommended Action

Oversecretion of histamines can be inhibited by using herbal antihistamines, however, one should change to a Cleansing Diet which is low in mucus to obtain long-term relief. Cleansing herbs are beneficial in ridding the body of any accumulated mucus and drinking steam-distilled or reverse osmosis water

Allergies: a multifactorial issue

Allergies or sensitivities are often multifactorial, that is, they are caused by many different factors simultaneously. It usually has to do with a critical threshold.

Let's say that a person has a 100-point threshold before having allergy symptoms. They might only have a 60-point allergic reaction to dairy products. Consuming dairy products won't trigger an allergic reaction by itself. Often other factors in a person's life will add "background" points. Let's say that they are under 30 points of stress, the weather contributes 20 points, another food sensitivity contributes 40 points. The accumulation of 150 points triggers symptoms. In this case, usually a buildup of mucus. Some factors can accumulate by themselves. Perhaps the body can only eliminate 30 points of allergic sensitivity to dairy per day. After 3-4 days of dairy consumption, the accumulation is more than 100 with the dairy alone.

Allergy Testing

There are many ways to test for allergies. The two simplest ones that you can do at home are the (Coca Pulse Test) and a Kinesiology test. I have included both of these in the Appendix section of this book.

increases the effects of both diet and herbs. See specific conditions (sinus, respiratory, skin, etc.) for relief from these symptoms. Often many allergies disappear when the body is cleaned out. Clean lungs, with little mucus, usually stop lung allergies. Food allergies are often alleviated if the digestive system is restored to full capacity with a clean colon. Skin eruptions can be aided by cleansing the blood and colon.

Single Herbs Reishi, Alfalfa (nutritive and to balance hyperacidity); Ma Huang herb (natural antihistamine and cleanser); Chaparral, Burdock Root or Comfrey (cleansers); Bee Pollen (reported to build up immunity to allergens when taken orally in very small but gradually increasing amounts); Horseradish root (a very fast-acting antihistamine); Parsley, Raspberry (eliminates mucus from the system).

Combinations Reishi Plus Formula, Parsley and Raspberry leaf (equal parts in a tea); Lung Formula (for respiratory allergies); Stomach Formula, Digestive Enzymes (food allergies); Lower Bowel Tonic (to keep the colon active) and Cleansing Formula.

Synergistic Vitamins and Minerals Beta-CEZB$_6$ (2 tablets, twice daily), Digestive Enzymes (1-3 capsules at each meal to aid in digestion), Beta-carotene (20,000-50,000 IU, twice daily), B complex (1 tablet, twice daily), Vitamin C (500 mg, six times daily), Calcium.

Suggested Program

Breakfast Digestive Enzymes (1-3 capsules), Lung Formula (2-3 capsules), Reishi Plus Formula (2-3 capsules), Ester C (500 mg), Beta-CEZB$_6$ (2 tablets)
Snack Ester C (500 mg)
Lunch Digestive Enzymes (1-3 capsules)
Snack as morning
Supper as Breakfast

Alzheimer's

(See Memory)

Amoebic Dysentery

In this condition the intestinal tract becomes invaded by *Entamoeba histolytica*, a parasitical microorganism which is usually transmitted by contaminated foods or liquids. The symptoms include diarrhea, abdominal pain, fever, lack of appetite and general weakness, with blood and mucus being visible in the stool in severe cases. If all these symptoms are present, it means the parasites have multiplied to such an extent as to have caused abscesses, ulcers or tumors in the lower intestines. If they migrate to other organs, such as the stomach or liver, it is possible for severe complications to result. If they become encysted, they will be difficult to reach and remove. This disease is most common in areas with poor sanitation, such as the tropics, although carriers may be found virtually anywhere.

Recommended Action

The diarrhea can be relieved by use of demulcent and astringent herbs, while the parasites can be dealt with specifically by use of garlic (taken orally and/or as an enema). Even encysted amoeba will be removed by the use of garlic over a period of time.

Single Herbs Goldenseal, Barberry, *Artemisia spp.*, Garlic.

Combinations Huang Lian Su (Berberini HCl), Parasite Formula, Goldenseal Plus Formula, Curing Pills, Psyllax.

Anemia

There are many types of anemia, which is basically a blood disorder. All forms result in weakness, fatigue, loss of appetite, aches and pains, heart and breathing difficulties, and the characteristic paleness of anemia. Anemia is due to a lack of oxygen reaching the various body tissues. This can be caused by not enough hemoglobin (oxygen-carrying substance in the blood) or not enough erythrocytes (red blood cells). Hemolytic anemia (involving the destruction of red blood cells) can occur as an allergic response to drugs or transfused blood. Rh factor anemia and sickle-cell anemia are inherited. Aplastic anemia (insufficient or incomplete bone marrow producing red blood cells) is caused by too many X-rays, radiation treatment or drug and chemical poisoning. Iron deficiency anemia usually results from an iron-poor diet or through not digesting and absorbing iron, but may also be caused by an excessive loss of blood. A lack of certain nutritional elements, such as Vitamin B_{12}, B_6, folic acid or lack of HCl in the stomach, can cause anemia as they are essential to the development of red blood cells. Iron is located at the core of the hemoglobin molecule and is responsible for binding with oxygen in order to carry it throughout the body. Hemoglobin accounts for 65% of the body's iron.

Recommended Action

Adding iron to the diet, either as a supplement or through foods such as whole grains (which are rich in manganese), will benefit iron-deficient anemia. The most absorbable form of iron is heme-iron, which is found in the blood of animal tissue. Iron can often be built up quickly by eating fish, meat especially rare steak. Copper and Vitamin C are required to absorb and retain iron. Vitamin B_{12} is necessary to deal with pernicious anemia and can be found in animal protein, fish, dairy products, sea vegetation and naturally fermented foods (sauerkraut, yogurt, and miso). Digestive enzymes, intrinsic factor and calcium are in turn required in order to assimilate B_{12}.

Single Herbs Beet powder, Chlorella, Yellow Dock and Alfalfa; Herbal Iron, Organic Iron; Comfrey (blood cleanser and cell proliferant); Dandelion root and Siberian Ginseng (blood builders); Kelp, Alfalfa and Barberry root bark (vitamins and minerals).

Combinations Cleansing Formula, Liver Formula, Stomach Formula, Digestive Enzymes (if lack of digestive enzymes is suspected).

Synergistic Vitamins and Minerals B complex, Vitamin B_6, Pantothenic acid, Folic acid, PABA, Vitamin E, Bone Meal, Vitamin C, Organic Iron. Also helpful are desiccated liver, beet juice, crude blackstrap molasses, sesame seed, and Digestive Enzymes (promotes assimilation of iron and Vitamin B_{12}).

Suggested Program

Breakfast Herbal Iron (1-2 tbsp), Organic Iron (15-30 mg), B complex (1 tablet), Ester C (500 mg), Digestive Enzymes (1-2 capsules), Chlorella (1,500 mg).
Lunch Ester C (500 mg), Four Ginsengs (2-3 capsules)
Supper Same as Breakfast.

Angina Pectoris

This condition, which can feel similar to a heart attack, lasts only a few minutes. It is characterized by chest pains that may be felt as only a mild tightness or pressure, or may be so extreme as to produce intense aching. Sometimes, too, pain can radiate from the chest to the shoulder and down the left arm. These pains are a result of the heart tissue not receiving enough oxygen (due to a diminished blood supply from the coronary arteries) and are often quickly relieved by rest. This is known as myocardial ischemia and is generally caused by arteriosclerosis of the coronary arteries. For a first-time sufferer, the distinct resemblance to a heart attack will generally result in great anxiety. Once aware of the condition, the sufferer can easily deal with it, lessening the overall anxiety experienced.

George's chest problem

George T., a 55 year old business man, came in suffering from chest pains on a regular basis. His medical doctor had diagnosed angina pectoris. After a discussion it was learned that he most often had "attacks" after the evening meal. It came up that he was having a lot of problems with his teenage son. About two hours after eating a big meal that wasn't digesting properly, he would get a chest pain. We suggested Reishi Plus Formula, cayenne and Digestive Enzymes. His chest problem disappeared within days. Reishi for anxiety, stress and circulation; cayenne for heart and circulation; Digestive Enzymes to stop gas formation.

Recommended Action

The person should immediately attempt to relax both mentally and physically. This will help put an end to the pain as the relaxed heart muscle will cause the blood vessels to dilate (open), decreasing the need for oxygen while increasing the heart's ability to pump blood and deliver oxygen. Adopting a diet low in sodium and high in potassium and adding fresh fruits and vegetables to the diet are essential for long-term relief. Muscle tone and blood vessel flexibility are improved through the use of Vitamin E and lecithin, while the entire circulatory system is strengthened by the use of Vitamin C and natural B complex vitamins. Potassium is absolutely essential to proper heart function. Garlic is effective both as an anti-atherosclerotic, preventing buildup of deposits on the artery wall, and as a vasodilator by opening the blood vessels. It should be noted that many apparent angina or heart attacks are really gas attacks. The pressure of gas in the intestine being strong enough to cause pain in the chest.

Single Herbs Lobelia Extract (relaxant); Elderberry Extract (potassium); Hawthorn Berry tincture (heart food and strengthener); Reishi, Cayenne or Cayenne Extract, Ginger (circulatory tonic and antiarteriosclerotic); Garlic, Kelp.

Combinations Nerve Formula (sedative, pain reliever), Cleansing Formula (cleanse blood to prevent recurrence), Reishi Plus Formula.

Synergistic Vitamins and Minerals Vitamin A, B complex with B_{12}, Vitamin B_{15} (N,N-Dimethylglycine and Calcium Gluconate, also referred to as Calcium Pangamate), Vitamin C, Vitamin E, Potassium, Calcium/Magnesium and Lecithin.

Suggested Program

Immediate supplements Lobelia Extract (10 drops), Cayenne Extract (20 drops), or 1/2 tsp. Cayenne pepper in water. Rest for a few days. Slowly increase exercise, such as walking and swimming. Adopt a diet low in sodium and high in potassium with an emphasis on whole grains, fruits, vegetables and a liberal use of garlic. No red meat and limited fowl and dairy products. No refined or processed foods. No sugar, white flour, coffee, tobacco or alcohol. Fish, sprouts, greens, and whole grains are the best foods to eat.

Breakfast Reishi Plus Formula (three), Elderberry Extract (1/2 tsp), Hawthorn Plus Formula (2-3 capsules), Vitamin E (400 IU), one B complex, Vitamin B_{15} (50 mg), Vitamin A (10,000 IU), Cayenne Plus Formula (one capsule in middle of meals), Calcium/Magnesium (200/100 mg), Vitamin C (500 mg), two Cleansing Formula.

Morning Snack Vitamin C (500 mg).

Lunch Hawthorn Plus Formula (2-3 capsules), Vitamin E (400 IU), Cayenne Plus Formula (one capsule in middle of meals), Ester C (500 mg), two Reishi Plus Formula.

Mid afternoon snack Ester C (500 mg).

Supper Same as breakfast.

Note: Vitamin E should start at 100 IU daily if it has not been used recently, gradually building up to recommended dosage. Make sure bowels are clean.

Appendicitis

This condition occurs when the appendix, a short finger-like projection about three inches long attached to the cecum (lower end of the ascending colon), becomes inflamed. Natural health practitioners feel the function of the appendix is to aid in lubrication of the ascending colon. The fecal matter can therefore make the upward trip more easily after entering from the small intestine. The inflammation generally results from some obstruction which is usually caused by constipation or faulty digestion. Pain, generally beginning near the navel, will soon spread to the lower right abdomen and be accompanied by loss of appetite, fever and possibly vomiting or diarrhea. Untreated inflammation may result in a ruptured appendix, causing the infection to spread into the abdominal cavity. This is often fatal.

Recommended Action

Take no solid food, drink plenty of liquid and take orally the same herbs as listed below for the enema. They work best in the form of a tea, mixed with fruit juices, or an alkaline (vegetable) broth. Olive oil is beneficial, either added to the enema and/or taken orally to assist in lubricating the colon and removing the obstruction. Demulcent herbs especially those for glands can be made into a healing poultice or fomentation to apply to the affected area repeatedly. It is very important in appendicitis to refrain from using any laxative as this may make the situation even more serious. This is especially true in the case of children, as their tissue is more delicate and more easily ruptured.

Captain Roberts suggests one teaspoon of Fluid Extract of Wild Yam in a wineglass of water, one teaspoon Tincture Echinacea in a wineglass of water, and a teaspoon of olive oil taken alternately. He also suggests olive oil rubbed freely into the lower right abdomen.

Single Herbs Chickweed, Elder flowers, Mullein (hot poultice with Lobelia and Ginger), Lady's Slipper root powder (1 teaspoon with 1/2 teaspoon Lobelia herb powder, steep for a few minutes in one cup of water); Echinacea (homeopathic), Ginseng (homeopathic). Coffee enemas can be useful also.

Combinations Goldenseal Plus Formula.

Appetite, Poor

There are many factors that can cause a poor appetite. Stress, depression and trauma are high on the list of underlying factors. Sometimes controllable factors are involved: alcohol, cigarette, or drug abuse. Poor appetite can also indicate a underlying chronic or acute disease, inflammation, heavy metal toxicity, or nutrition deficiency. It may be a side effect of pharmaceutical drugs. Low stomach acids or poor digestive enzymes might also be the cause. An excessive sedentary lifestyle can also be a contributing factor.

Recommended Action

The most important thing to do is to find the underlying factor. For this you might have to consult with a health practitioner. Get them to check out the above possibilities as well as eating disorders. For someone with poor appetite, large amounts of food can often be disheartening. Start with frequent small meals, slowly working up to larger proportions. Digestive enzymes, B complex and zinc can often help. Consider the appearance and aroma of the food as well as the environment the food is eaten in.

Single Herbs Gentian, Dandelion (Bitters), Catnip, Fennel Seed, Ginger root, Mints (calming to the digestive tract).

Combinations Digestive Enzymes, Stomach Formula, Liver Formula.

Synergistic Vitamins and Minerals Beta-CEZB$_6$ (2 tablets, twice daily), Beta-carotene (20,000 IU), B complex (50 mg, twice daily), Vitamin B$_{12}$ (1,000 mcg daily), Zinc (30-80 mg), Copper (3 mg).

Suggested Program

Breakfast Digestive enzymes (1-3 capsules, depending on size and density of meal), Stomach Formula (1-2 capsules), B complex (50 mg), Zinc (15-30 mg)
Lunch Digestive enzymes (1-3 capsules), Stomach Formula (1-2 capsules)
Supper same as breakfast with maybe an aperitif, such as Campari or Angostura Bitters (if not contraindicated by other health issues).

Brothy soups can be beneficial in these cases, especially "bone soups".

Arteriosclerosis

This condition involves the buildup of calcium deposits (calcification) on the inside of the artery walls, causing thickening and hardening (sclerosis) of the artery. If the deposits are fatty substances (atheromas), the condition is properly referred to as atherosclerosis. However, both conditions have about the same effect on circulation. High blood pressure (hypertension) is commonly associated with arteriosclerosis and can cause this condition or, conversely, this condition can cause high blood pressure. The deposits, whether calcium or fatty substances, tend to form in the areas of the arteries that have been weakened by high blood pressure or strain. Narrowing of the arteries forces already high blood pressure even higher. As the arteries become less pliable and less penetrable, ischemia (cell starvation) results due to insufficient circulation to the cells. There is a danger of heart attack, apoplexy or stroke, especially in older people. These are caused when one of the coronary arteries becomes completely obstructed by accumulated deposits or by a blood clot either formed or snagged on the deposit.

Recommended Action

To strengthen the heart and clean out the artery walls, implement an exercise program, starting slowly and gradually increasing to aerobic activity. The diet should be changed to eliminate all refined starches, white flour, sugar and saturated fats. Reducing the intake of saturated animal fats and animal proteins will help prevent atheromas, which contains high amounts of lipids (fat-related products such as cholesterol and triglycerides). Salt should also be eliminated. Lecithin, Vitamin C and B complex should be added to the diet as ethey will assist in reducing lipid levels in the blood and in strengthening blood vessels.

Single Herbs Reishi, Cayenne, Garlic, Ginger, Siberian Ginseng (antiatherosclerotics and circulatory tonics); Alfalfa (especially the sprouts), Dandelion, Chlorella, Black Radish.

Combinations Reishi Plus Formula (3 capsules, 3 times daily), Cleansing Formula (two, twice daily), Chorella (1,250 mg, twice daily).

Synergistic Vitamins and Minerals B complex with extra niacin, Vitamin B_6, Inositol and Choline, Vitamin C, Vitamin E, Calcium, Magnesium, Chromium and Lecithin.

Suggested Program

Breakfast Reishi Plus Formula (3 capsules), Cleansing Formula (2 capsules), Garlic (2 capsules), Beta-CEZB_6 (2 tablets), B complex (1 tablet), Niacin (50-100 mg), Multivitamins (2 tablets).
Snack Ester C (500 mg)
Lunch Reishi Plus Formula (3 capsules), Ester C (500 mg)
Snack same as morning
Supper same as Breakfast

Drink 1-4 cups of ginger root tea daily.

Arthritis

Arthritis is basically an inflammation of the joints and presents itself in a variety of ways, the two most common being rheumatoid arthritis and osteoarthritis. The former attacks the synovial membranes surrounding the lubricating fluid in the joints and creates stiffness, swelling and often crippling pain. The latter, known as degenerative joint disease, is related to the wear and tear of aging and involves deterioration of the cartilage ends of the bones. This second type usually involves much less pain and little or no swelling. Gout, which occurs more often in overweight people and those who indulge regularly in rich foods and alcohol, is another form of arthritis. It usually occurs in the smaller joints of the feet and hands, generally affecting the big toe. Deposits of crystallized uric acid salt in the joint cause swelling, redness, and a sensation of heat and extreme pain.

Yes, arthritis can be reversed

Mrs G., a 56 year old women, came into the clinic with swollen joints, and reduced mobility due to arthritis. By following the accompanying program with the diet in the Appendix, she noticed some relief within 6 weeks. After 6 months she was virtually symptom-free, losing 35 pounds as a side benefit.

Recommended Action

Drink steam-distilled water daily and take a generous portion of herbs capable of dissolving organic deposits of calcium and mineral salts responsible for the symptoms of arthritis. Anchovies, sardines, beef and internal organs of animals (such as kidneys and liver) are all rich in purine (a substance involved in the production of uric acid) and should therefore be avoided by anyone with gouty arthritis. Follow a good natural diet and use periodic juice fasting or Cleansing Diets to help this condition improve.

Single Herbs Cat's Claw, Chaparral, Devil's Claw, Devil's Club, Hydrangea, Irish Moss, Yucca (for dissolving inorganic deposits); Alfalfa, Dandelion root, Comfrey, Licorice root, Bee Pollen (organic nutrients); Saffron (for dissolving uric salts in Gout); Aloe Vera gel or juice, Red Clover, Dulse.

Combinations Arthritis Formula; Bone, Flesh and Cartilage (for dissolving inorganic deposits); Nerve Formula, Trauma Ointment (pain relief); Cleansing Formula, Lower Bowel Tonic (cleanser and eliminator).

Synergistic Vitamins and Minerals Vitamin A, B complex with B_{12}, Vitamin B_6, Niacin, Pantothenic acid, Vitamin C, Vitamin E, Calcium, Magnesium, Trace Minerals, Cod or Halibut Liver Oil.

Suggested Program

Follow Arthritis diet (see Appendix).

One hour before breakfast take one tablespoon of Cod or Halibut Liver oil. This can be mixed with 2 tablespoons of orange juice or milk. Nothing else, including water, should be taken for half an hour.

Breakfast Take one tablespoon of apple cider vinegar with one teaspoon of honey in one-third to one cup of warm water at the beginning of breakfast. Take Arthritis Formula (2-3 capsules), one B complex, Vitamin C (500 mg), Calcium/Magnesium (2 tablets), one Multiminerals, Digestive Enzymes (1-3 capsules depending on need). Rub Trauma Ointment or Inflammation Ointment into sore areas.

Morning Snack Ester C (500 mg).

Lunch Arthritis Formula (2-3 capsules), Ester C (500 mg), Aloe Vera (1/4 cup), Vitamin E (400 IU).

Afternoon Snack Ester C (500 mg).

Supper Same as breakfast.

Evening Cod or Halibut liver oil, as taken before breakfast.

Note: Make sure bowels are clean. If they are not, take Lower Bowel Tonic.

Asthma

Asthma is a type of allergic reaction which attacks the respiratory system and is characterized by labored breathing, coughing, wheezing and often a feeling of suffocation. The allergens which can cause asthma generally include such things as dust, pollen, animal hairs, foods and various chemical substances found in both processed foods and air. However, asthmatic attacks may also be set off by emotional stress, as this lessens the bodies resistance and increases its sensitivity to allergens in the environment. During an asthma attack, a muscle spasm causes the bands of involuntary muscles, which surround the bronchioles (small air passages in the lungs), to constrict. Consequently, the flow of air to the alveoli (tiny air sacs within the lungs) is also restricted. This is often accompanied by the simultaneous swelling of the lining of the air passages, with excessive secretion of mucus into these passages. All these combine to cause even more difficulty. In an effort to expel mucus from the air passages, the body initiates asthmatic coughing, while the wheezing sound comes from air travelling over pockets of mucus in the passages causing them to resonate. Chronic wheezing, not accompanied by asthmatic attacks, could indicate a dietary problem involving excessive amounts of mucus-forming foods and is often accompanied by a mild nervous condition. There is also clinical evidence linking asthma to hypoglycemia.

Asthma is often internalization of stress

Have you ever watched an emotional scene in a movie and catch yourself holding your breath? Some asthmatic people chronically hold in tension in a similar way. By creating circular arguments in their head, they tend to tighten up their chest muscles and the round muscles of their respiratory tract. Reishi has been very useful for releasing the underlying stress. This is particularly so in situations involving young boys. Reishi has been the single most important herb for treating asthma in boys who are 6-15 years old.

Recommended Action

For acute attacks take a cup of Elder flower or Elderberry tea follow this by a 1/4 tsp. of Lobelia Extract and/or Ma Huang tea or extract as it is also beneficial in relaxing the bronchial muscles. In order to obtain long-term relief it is necessary to remove all mucus-forming foods from the diet. The following supplements are also extremely beneficial:

1. Vitamin A for healthy lungs.
2. B complex to strengthen the nervous system.
3. Vitamin C to combat stress factors.
4. Calcium to relax and rebuild the nerves.
5. Potassium to inhibit mucus production.

It is also helpful to use relaxant herbs to prevent constriction of the bronchial muscles, and expectorant herbs to help release and expel mucus. Ephedrine is often used in medical treatment as a bronchiodilator (opens up air passages), as is adrenalin. Cortisone is also used in conventional therapy to stimulate adrenal activity. Some natural herbal substitutes for these remedies would be Ma Huang and Licorice root (which stimulates the adrenals). It is also beneficial to keep the living area, and especially the sleeping area, quite humid. A vaporizer or humidifier is good and will act as a mild bronchiodilator if you put a few drops of eucalyptus oil in it.

Single Herbs Ma Huang (bronchiodilator); Cat's Claw, Licorice root (expectorant and adrenal stimulant); Slippery Elm, Comfrey, Mullein (demulcents, expectorants, specifics for lungs); Elderberry Extract (potassium, anti-mucus); Lobelia Extract (relaxant, emetic and expectorant); Bee Pollen (see Allergies); Garlic (expectorant).

Combinations Lung Formula, Reishi Plus Formula.

Synergistic Vitamins and Minerals Beta-CEZB$_6$, Vitamin A, B complex, Vitamin C, Vitamin D, Vitamin E, Calcium, Magnesium, Manganese.

Asthma Case Study

In the case of bronchial, asthmatic and many other lung problems we have found Ma Huang to be an excellent herb but it is best regulated as in the Lung Formula. Mrs. V. from Prince Albert, Sask., had such bad asthma that she couldn't sleep properly at nights: "I felt as if I was drowning". But following the outlined program, within a week she could sleep at night and in one and a half months she was breathing normally again. After ten months of following the program she was symptom-free, without the supplements, as long as she didn't eat mucus-forming foods.

Suggested Program

Start the program with a 12 day D-tox Diet or a 7-14 day Inner Cleanse Diet, while avoiding all mucus-forming foods. Diet should emphasize garlic, green vegetables and fresh fruits. Manganese-rich foods are also advisable, some of which are peas, beans, blueberries, nuts and buckwheat. Alternating hot and cold showers have been found quite successful. Take a 3-5 minute hot shower, switching immediately to a cold shower (as cold as possible) for 10-15 seconds. Repeat three times, always ending with a cold shower. Of course plenty of aerobic exercise in clean, non-smoggy air is beneficial.

Supplements

Breakfast Lung Formula (2-3 capsules), Reishi Plus Formula (3 capsules), Beta-CEZB$_6$ (2 tablets), Calcium/Magnesium (1 tablet), Vitamin E (400 IU), two Garlic capsules, Manganese (5 mg, twice a week for 10 weeks).

Morning Snack Ester C (500 mg).

Lunch Lung Formula (2-3 capsules), Ester C (500 mg), Calcium/Magnesium (1 tablet), Vitamin A (20,000 IU).

Afternoon Snack Ester C (500 mg).

Supper Same as breakfast.

Attention Deficit Disorder (ADD)

also known as hyperactivity disorder

This syndrome is the inability to pay attention, concentrate, remember, think clearly, with emotional instability and learning problems. Most of the patients I've seen with this problem are above average intelligence, but just can't do well at organized tasks. Often there will be some things (like Lego® or computer games) that they can concentrate on for long periods of time. It almost appears that they are bored with their environment. We can really divide this area down into three groups: attention deficit disorder without hyperactivity (more common in female children); attention deficit disorder with hyperactivity (more common in male children 10:1); attention deficit disorder - residual type (most common as an extension of earlier problems after the 18th year).

ADD and Reishi

The most important herb for ADD is Reishi. It has performed such wonders for children that I have had more than one teacher phone me up, thanking me for helping their student. Reishi seems to calm down some of the internal babble going on inside their head. It also helps lower their susceptibility to allergies.

The causes of these disorders are not completely understood, but some of the factors that contribute are: heredity, smoking while pregnant, oxygen deprivation or trauma at birth, artificial food additives, sugar, dairy, environmental pollutants, lead poisoning, food sensitivities. Food containing dye (especial red dye), preservatives, added sugar or salicylates seem to be the biggest causes.

Recommended Action

The most important thing to do is to concentrate on the diet. We remove all sugars, dairy and additives. This is a little bit of a problem, not only in the convenience for the food preparer, but because the child is often addicted to these foods. We have found if you can't get the child to "buy in" on the program, it is next to impossible to administer. Sometimes it is hard to remember that underneath the "little monster" there is an intelligent child who also needs self-respect.

I have found variation of the following themes to work. Have the child follow the diet for two weeks. At the end of this time take the whole family bowling, as a kind of reward. Bowling is fairly kinesthetic, with a need for concentration. If a child hasn't bowled that much, they will probably get better with each game. Plan on bowling three games. Halfway through the second game, let the child eat all the wrong foods: sugar, pizza, soda pop containing red dye, etc. Almost immediately they will not be able to concentrate during bowling. It wouldn't be surprising to see them only able to hit the gutter of their lane. They will probably start throwing a fit. Ask them to focus inside themselves to see if they feel comfortable.

It appears that an ADD child feels confused and uncomfortable inside. They create a scene outside themselves, often as a mechanism to distract themselves from their inner confusion. After consuming the wrong foods, they will usually say they don't feel good. Point out that the foods they just ate are probably responsible. In fact, you might say that they seem to be allergic to those foods. I have seen athletic children lose all coordination after consuming red dye and/or sugar. Often a variation on this experiment has to be repeated every three to six months, to remind the child. ADD children are usually intelligent enough that they will try the experiment on their own also ... just to be sure. Unfortunately with ADD, it is almost always a battle between an addiction, on the one hand, and a food sensitivity, on the other. If strong compliance to this program is achieved, good results will be possible.

Often after being off a food group for 2-4 months the child can consume it once to twice a week on "special occasions". The following supplements are all useful but a practitioner should be involved to monitor dosage levels.

Single Herbs Reishi, Valerian, Wild Oats (*Avena*).

Combinations Reishi Plus Formula, Valerian Plus Formula.

Synergistic Vitamins and Minerals Beta-CEZB$_6$ (1-2 tablets, twice daily), Beta-carotene (20,000 IU, twice daily), Vitamin B$_6$ (25-50 mg daily), Vitamin C (500-2,000 mg daily), Multivitamins and minerals (1 tablet, twice daily), SAF for Kids (1-2 capsules, two to three times daily), Calcium (200-800 mg daily), Magnesium (100-400mg daily), Zinc (2-30 mg daily), GABA (gamma-amino butyric acid, has been found useful).

Suggested Program

Breakfast Reishi (2-3 capsules), Beta-CEZB_6 (1 tablet), Multivitamins and minerals (1 tablet), SAF for Kids (1-2 capsules).
Lunch same as breakfast if indicated
Supper often switched with lunch, but if indicated a third repeat of breakfast.

Bedwetting

Unconscious wetting during sleep by a person over the age of three is clinically termed enuresis, while involuntary urination by a child or adult during waking hours is referred to as incontinence. Infection or inflammation of the urinary tract, worms or other irritants, general weakness and debility, extreme tiredness, drinking too much liquid, eating spicy food which irritates the urinary tract and emotional stress can all cause this problem.

Recommended Action

Refined foods should be eliminated from the diet as they weaken the system. Eat the evening meal no later than 4 or 5 o'clock and do not eat again before bedtime. Especially do not consume liquid the last few hours before bedtime. If thirsty, eat fresh fruit, but only if absolutely necessary. Immediately upon arising give plenty of liquids so as to dilute the strength of retained urine. Many cases of enuresis are of an emotional nature. If the parents are confronted in the child's presence with the statement that the child is merely doing it for attention, they will usually state that their child gets all the attention that he/she needs. At some subconscious level the child seems to realize that they do indeed get attention, and the enuresis will often cease shortly thereafter.

Single Herbs Uva Ursi, Juniper berries, Buchu, Parsley leaves, Cat's Claw.

Combinations Kidney Formula, Reishi Plus Formula, Parsley/ Raspberry leaf tea.

Synergistic Vitamins and Minerals Vitamin A (10,000 IU, twice daily), B complex, Vitamin C (1500 mg, three times daily), Multivitamins and minerals.

Bladder Infection

See Kidney and Bladder.

Bleeding

Bleeding usually refers to the external loss of blood from a blood vessel, while hemorrhage usually refers to the rupture of an internal blood vessel. External bleeding can involve a wide range of severity and include such things as abrasions (scrapes), lacerations (tears), punctures (such as stabbing) or gunshot wounds. In less severe wounds, involving broken or severed capillaries, the blood will flow momentarily in order to wash out the wound, and within a few minutes a clot will begin to form. In more severe wounds, involving a severed vein or artery, the flow of blood will be stronger and more profuse.

Cayenne can stop bleeding fast

Taking a teaspoon of cayenne pepper in water can stop bleeding from a wound within 15-30 seconds. How does it do this? I don't know. The chemicals in cayenne can't even get to the wound site in that amount of time. Another one of those mysteries of nature.

Arterial blood is bright red because it contains a high amount of oxygen and is being pumped directly from the heart; it will flow in spurts. On the other hand, venous blood is darker because it is returning from the cells, carrying carbon dioxide rather than oxygen and not being pumped directly; it will flow more steadily. A bruise is an area of mild internal tissue damage where blood released from capillaries has accumulated. The change in color of a bruise from red or purple to brown, green or even yellow before completely disappearing directly results from the hemoglobin in the red blood cells breaking down as the blood elements rebuild the injured tissue.

Recommended Action

The best emergency measure for any bleeding, either internal or external, is a teaspoon of cayenne in a glass of warm water. If bleeding is internal, use a homeostatic herb that is a specific for the particular organ involved. Simmer it in one pint of milk, then drink it slowly. Cayenne will control the bleeding. Goldenseal, to prevent infection, may be applied directly to minor external wounds. Plantain, comfrey or yarrow (either fresh or powdered) are more beneficial for severe wounds (internal or external). In a case of arterial or venous bleeding, apply direct pressure around the wound and get immediate attention. Generally, bruises are not serious, however, if bruising occurs easily, it signifies fragile, or easily ruptured, blood vessels. This condition can be remedied with a good calcium supplement, and it is advisable to beware of Vitamin C deficiency. Large amounts of bioflavonoids are also usually needed.

Single Herbs Cayenne, Plantain, Comfrey, Yarrow (vulneraries); Goldenseal root (uterine homeostatic); Mullein (bowel and lungs); Marshmallow (bladder); Goldenseal, White Oak bark (nose); Gumweed ointment (prevents scarring).

Synergistic Vitamins and Minerals Vitamin A (20,000 IU), Vitamin C (1000-3000 mg), Vitamin E oil over scab area after healing has advanced, Bioflavonoids (250 mg, four - six times daily), Calcium (200 mg daily), Magnesium (100 mg daily), Trace Minerals.

Blood Pressure

See High or Low Blood Pressure.

Boils

see Abscess

Bowel and Colon

Proper functioning of the bowel and colon is essential to good health. The term "bowel" refers to both the large and small intestines, while "colon" refers only to the lower bowel or large intestine. The primary function of the colon is to absorb water and electrolytes and solidify the fecal matter prior to elimination from the body. The bulk of the nutrients is absorbed by the small intestine. Only a small amount of nutrients are absorbed in the ascending and transverse sections of the colon. Fecal deposits adhere to the walls of the intestine and solidify. They are a direct result of a rich diet and refined foods producing varying degrees of chronic constipation.

Normal bowel movements become difficult to impossible as the hardened deposits interfere with absorption and immobilize peristaltic muscles.

Constipation

Mrs. M. came into my clinic in 1986 with a constipation problem. I suggested Lower Bowel Tonic at a dosage of two capsules, three times daily. This normal dosage wasn't enough so we increased the dosage until she had one full bowel movement daily. Her dosage was an extraordinary four capsules, five times daily. Her biggest question was: ". . . won't I become dependent on these as I have on laxatives and enemas?". I assured her that this wasn't the case with the Lower Bowel Tonic. After one year she only needed twelve to have two movements daily; by two years it was down to six capsules, and by two years seven months she didn't need any to maintain one to two movements daily. Four years later, she only took the Lower Bowel Tonic if she had eaten a very big dinner or if she had eaten improperly for a while (she generally used about three - five a month). Now, she does 1-2 D-Tox Diets a year to cleanse out her bowel.

Recommended Action

Drink copious amounts of steam-distilled or reverse osmosis water and be sure to include plenty of fresh fruits, vegetables, whole grains, nuts and seeds in the diet. Supplementing with additional vegetable fiber may be necessary in some cases. Alfalfa sprouts or tablets are excellent. Lower Bowel Tonic is a good remedy to help rebuild immobilized peristaltic muscles. Highly refined starches and sugars should be eliminated entirely from the diet, while it is advisable to greatly reduce the intake of rich foods and mucus-forming foods, such as meat, eggs and dairy products. One of the most common herbs to use for colon problems is senna, however, long term use of it can become habit-forming.

Single Herbs Alfalfa, Cascara sagrada, Turkey Rhubarb.

Combinations Lower Bowel Tonic (3 capsules, 2-3 times daily); occasionally Senna and Ginger (3:1 ratio); Psyllax (acts as a bulking poultice for the intestinal tract); Chlorella (intestinal detoxifier and oxygenator).

Breast Problems

The most common problem in this area is fibrocystic breast disease (FBD), which is quite frequent (upwards of 50%) in adult females. Other problems can include breast cancer, though it is much less frequent. FBD can be hardly noticeable or produce severe pain. FBD is caused by benign lumps or fluid-filled cysts. These lumps usually give the most discomfort premenstrually or during menstruation. It was once thought that frequent FBD would increase the probability of breast cancer. This has proven to be incorrect. The cause usually has to do with the estrogen-progesterone ratio.

Recommended Action

Breast cysts are often linked to excessive caffeine, iodine deficiency, low thyroid function and high estrogen. A sluggish liver or constipation can also be related to the cause. We immediately suggest the person stop consumption of all methylxanthines (found in coffee, tea, cola, chocolate). Even decaffeinated coffee should be eliminated. A low fat diet (especially reduced dairy and commercial red meats) should be implemented. Organically-raised or wild game, and low fat yogurt, seem to be no problem for FBD patients. High fiber is also very important. Eat at least two servings of whole grain daily. Other substances to avoid are: large amounts of alcohol, cooking oils, rancid oils, fried food, tobacco and white flour. The most important supplements are the essential fatty acids (found in Evening Primrose oil, Borage or Currant oils). Fish oils also seem quite good. A poultice of poke root applied to the breast has been found beneficial.

Caffeine and Fibrocystic Breast

The number one cause of FBD is the consumption of caffeine. By stopping coffee, tea, cola, chocolate and other caffeine-containing foods, while consuming plenty of Essential Fatty Acids, more than 60% of breast cysts will be reduced, if not eliminated.

Single Herbs Essential fatty acids as found in Evening Primrose, Borage, Currant Oils; Dandelion root, Kelp, Dong Quai, Goldenseal root, Poke root poultice.

Combinations Essential Oil Blend, Female Formula; if indicated, Lower Bowel Tonic and Liver Formula and/or Digestive Enzymes. If inflammation, Goldenseal Plus Formula.

Synergistic Vitamins and Minerals Beta-CEZB$_6$ (2 tablets, twice daily), Iodine (0.25 mg daily), Beta-carotene (30,000 IU, twice daily), Vitamin C (3,000-7,000 mg, divided over the day), B complex (25-50 mg), Vitamin B$_6$ (100-500 mg daily), Vitamin E (400-800 IU daily), Zinc (15-50 mg daily), *Lactobacillus acidophilus*.

Breast Cysts

Mrs. N. came in with two large size cysts in her left breast. It was suggested that she take two Cleansing Formula (three times daily); two Female Formula (three times daily); Vitamin E (400 IU, twice daily) and Evening Primrose oil (2000 mg, twice daily); a low mucus diet with lots of freshly cooked whole grains and no caffeine. After a month the cysts had reduced in size substantially. After two months they were completely gone.

Suggested Program

Breakfast Female Formula (2-3 capsules), Beta-CEZB$_6$ (1-2 tablets), Essential Fatty Acids (1,000 - 3,000 mg), Kelp (500-1000 mg), B complex (25 mg ratio)
Snack Ester C (1,000 mg)
Lunch Essential Fatty Acids (1,000 - 2,000 mg), Ester C (1,000 mg), Vitamin E (400 IU)
Snack Ester C (1,000 mg)
Supper Same as Breakfast

The suggested diet is listed under Recommended Action. Apply poultice if needed. Homeopathic tissue salts such as Nat. Sulph. and Nat. Mur. 12X can be very beneficial in these cases.

Bronchitis

Bronchitis is any inflammation occurring in the mucous membrane which lines the bronchial tubes of the lungs. Coughing, wheezing, spitting up of mucus and difficulty breathing are all the usual symptoms. Acute bronchitis generally results as a complication of infection elsewhere in the respiratory tract, while chronic bronchitis results from protracted lung irritation (i.e., heavy smoking, air pollution or stubborn infection in the throat or lungs). Serious diseases such as emphysema, tuberculosis and lung cancer are usually preceded by bronchitis.

Recommended Action

Hot vapor or steam baths (especially with a little eucalyptus oil) facilitate dilation (opening) of the bronchial passages. Herbs of a demulcent and expectorant nature can be taken orally or applied as hot fomentations to the chest and thoracic area of the spine to obtain relief. If the condition is severe, it may be necessary to use an emetic which will bring up the excess mucus and relax the throat, stomach and bronchial passages. It is also important to cleanse the bowel and eliminate mucus-forming foods from the diet.

Single Herbs Ma Huang, Coltsfoot herb, Mullein, Comfrey, Lobelia, Cat's Claw, Marshmallow root, Gumweed.

Combinations Lung Formula, Reishi Plus Formula.

Synergistic Vitamins Beta-CEZB$_6$, Vitamin A, B complex, Vitamin C, Vitamin D, Vitamin E, Bioflavonoids, Iron, Manganese, Multivitamins and minerals.

Suggested Program

Breakfast Lung Formula (2-3 capsules), Beta-CEZB$_6$ (2 tablets), Goldenseal Plus Formula (2 capsules), Vitamin E (200 IU), Bioflavonoids (200 mg).
Morning Snack Vitamin C (500 mg), Elderberry Extract (1/2 tsp.), Lobelia extract (five drops).
Lunch Lung Formula (2 capsules), Vitamin C (500 mg).
Afternoon Snack Same as morning snack.
Supper Same as breakfast.

Bruises

Bruising happens when the underlying tissue is damaged, without surface skin being broken. It often results in painful swelling, accompanied by black and blue marks, caused by the accumulation of blood under the skin. Even though bruising can be the result of daily activity, like simply bumping into something, some people are more predisposed than others. Bruising is usually a condition of poor nutrition, especially lack of bioflavonoids. It can indicate a sluggish liver. Other things to rule out in the case of easy bruising are anaemia, excess weight, malnutrition, leukemia, and excessive use of anticlotting drugs.

Recommended Action

The most important thing to consider is adequate nutrition, especially plenty of Vitamin C, Bioflavonoids (especially rutin), vitamin K (high in leafy dark green vegetables). One suggestion is to add buckwheat and fresh vegetables to your diet. Stay away from aspirin-type drugs. If bruises continue, see a health practitioner.

Single Herbs Alfalfa, Chlorella.

Combinations Trauma Ointment, Inflammation Ointment.

Synergistic Vitamins and Minerals Vitamin C (3,000-10,000 mg throughout the day), Bioflavonoids (1,000-3,000 mg daily), *Lactobacillus acidophilus* (2 capsules, twice daily).

Burns

Burns are the result of exposure to extreme or prolonged heat causing different degrees of damage to the skin. Only the outer layer of skin is affected in first degree burns, which involve redness and discomfort but no actual blistering or destruction of flesh. The next layer of skin may be penetrated by second degree burns, which involves raised blisters, sometimes destroyed hair follicles and sweat glands and often serious infectious complications. Complete destruction of the skin tissue occurs in third degree burns, which involve damage to deeper tissues, leaving the skin either charred or whitened. Sunburns are usually only first degree but may sometimes be second degree burns. Although not severe, they cause great discomfort due to the large surface area they occupy. For serious burns or those covering a large area, medical aid should be sought immediately.

Recommended Action

Regardless of the degree of burn or scald, the best first aid to use is cold water to take the heat out. It is also important to guard against the complications of dehydration, shock and infection. For minor burns, after soaking the burn in cold water to return body temperature to normal, apply a healing salve like Trauma Ointment. Leave it on, only adding to it as necessary until the burn is entirely healed. Use straight Aloe Vera gel or alternate with a salve made of honey, wheat germ oil and olive oil, all of which make good burn salves. Honey salve, with equal parts of honey and wheat germ oil blended with powdered comfrey, is a very good remedy, but probably the best remedy is pure Aloe Vera gel or juice. Pain can be relieved by bathing with diluted apple cider vinegar, while Vitamin E oil is extremely beneficial to aid the rebuilding of burned tissue (don't put on burn until it has returned to body temperature). To prevent scarring once healing is under way, apply gumweed ointment or calendula ointment.

PABA, a B vitamin, taken internally or applied locally, will help prevent sunburn. Sunblock Protection Factor (SPF) relates to the amount of time it takes to get a sunburn. Products carrying SPF 5 claim to reduce burning so that a sunburn would occur in a period five times longer than normal. SPF 15 is generally considered the maximum effective protection, even though products with higher ratings can be purchased. Do not use Vitamin E on burns that are infected or when there is risk of infection, as it can interfere with the infection-fighting ability of the white blood cells.

Single Herbs Aloe Vera gel, Comfrey ointment, Gumweed ointment.

Combination Trauma Ointment.

Synergistic Vitamins and Minerals Vitamin A (10,000-20,000 IU), B complex, PABA (50-100 mg), Vitamin C (3000-5000 mg), Vitamin E (800 IU) plus topical application, Zinc (10 mg).

Aloe works

I was out at my cabin one fall cutting firewood for the winter. I had been chain sawing for about five hours, my arms were quite sore and the chainsaw was very hot. In one of those great moments of complete clumsiness I leaned my hand down onto the exhaust of the saw. My hand started to cook immediately. Before I knew what had happened my right hand had a very severe burn. I immediately soaked my hand in cold water, which, of course, brought the temperature down and gave some quick but very short-lived relief. I then started to prepare an Aloe Vera bath. To do this I put enough Aloe to completely cover my hand into a stainless steel bowl. This bowl I placed into another much larger bowl which was filled with ice. Instant pain relief, but as soon as I took my hand out of the Aloe ... instant pain. After several hours of keeping my hand immersed in the Aloe and pain-free (with much pain if I dared lift it out again), I eventually figured out how to sleep leaving my hand in the Aloe. I bandaged my hand up in Aloe drenched gauze. My burn healed in what I considered record time with no lack of movement or scarring.

Bursitis

The synovial bursa are small fluid-filled sacs whose function is to prevent friction between the parts of a joint. Bursitis is the inflammation of this sac. Injury or infection is generally responsible for acute bursitis while chronic bursitis may or may not have obvious causes. Some calcium deposits are inevitably revealed in the troublesome joint when X-rays are taken. Congestion in the transverse colon seems to be associated with bursitis in the neck and shoulder.

Recommended Action

Short-term relief of symptomatic pain can be achieved through the use of fomentations and liniments (Arnica and Cayenne Tincture) and/or Trauma Ointment. However, a thorough cleansing program and a diet low in mucus are necessary to correct the problem.

Single Herbs Devil's Claw, Yucca, Cayenne, Arnica tincture, Cod Liver Oil. Essential fatty acids like Evening Primrose Oil, Borage Oil, etc.

Combinations Arthritis Formula, Nerve Formula, Inflammation Ointment, Lower Bowel Tonic (if constipation associated).

Synergistic Vitamins and Minerals Vitamin A, B complex with B_{12} and B_6, Niacin, Pantothenic Acid, Vitamin C, Vitamin D, Vitamin E, Calcium, Magnesium, Trace Minerals, Cod or Halibut Liver Oil, Lecithin.

Suggested Program

Follow program for arthritis with Arthritis Diet. Add to the program one capsule of cayenne in the middle of breakfast and supper.

Candida

The Candida diet needs to be strict

Unfortunately you have to be completely strict on the Candida diet (see Appendix). I consider a Candida colony to be like a bunch of drug addicts. If you keep drugs away from addicts, but let them have drugs on Friday nights, it won't discourage them. By eating sweets (or other cheat foods) while on the Candida program you will not only continue to feed the yeast, you will create a stronger strain. Cheating is not allowed, unless prepared for. Once every four months you can use Berberini HCl (3 tablets, three times daily) and cheat for two weeks. We like to keep this for special occasions, like Christmas or that cruise you have been saving up for.

Candida albicans or common yeast is present in most people. A small harmless amount in the gastrointestinal tact is of no concern. It becomes a problem when it multiplies, creating extensive colonies. Overgrowth can have a profound effect on the immune system and be an underlying cause of a multitude of other health conditions. Some of these complaints can be very obvious such as thrush, vaginitis, athletes foot and jock itch. Still others, like irritable bowel syndrome (IBS), colitis, food sensitivities, fatigue, decreased libido, rectal itching, bladder infection, ear infection, abdominal bloating, heartburn, depression, acne and even auto immune diseases may seem unrelated. We have noticed a very big increase in the amount of yeast infection over the last several years. In the late 70's and early 80's we saw few cases, but now in the mid-90's, it is one of the most common problems we see.

Candida does affect both males and female, even though it is more common in females. It is rarely transmitted sexually however it can be transmitted by a mother to a newborn. It appears that it has more to do with an individual's immune function, than anything else. If a person's immune system is even slightly compromised, the yeast gains a foothold and can easily multiply.

It is not known why we have a higher incidence of yeast or Candida problems these days. Some feel that the yeast itself is stronger and that excessive use of antibiotic, steroidal compounds (including corticosteroids, oral contraceptives and hormone replacement therapy) has contributed to Candida's overall abundance. Many pharmaceuticals will kill other organisms that can keep the yeast in check, while some pharmaceuticals actually feed the yeast. Lack of proper digestive enzymes and overconsumption of sugar can certainly play a significant role in the increase of yeast.

Recommended Action

The most important factor to keep Candida under control is diet (see Candida diet in the Appendix). A very strict compliance to this diet is necessary. Most of the anti-fungal agents like Nystatin®, will weaken the immune system and are therefore not recommended. They might appear to give short term success, but usually drive the yeast deeper into the body. A person should try to avoid steroidal compounds like corticosteroid, oral contraceptives and antibiotics while on a Candida diet.

One of the most important areas to consider is digestion. If the food is not being digested properly, it will ferment in the digestive tract and be a perfect breeding ground for the yeast. Constipation can also be a contributing factor. The bowels must be kept clean. The use of anything that might compromise the immune system should be avoided or at least reduced. Liver function is important to watch in the battle against yeast. A sluggish liver will definitely increase yeast growth. Conversely, a yeast growth will often cause a sluggish liver. This will often result in all kinds of skin problems such as rashes or eczema. Stress can also increase the yeast rather rapidly.

We normally start off all Candida programs with a 12 day D-Tox Diet (see Appendix). This usually will help us gain a 1-2 month headstart on the Candida program. It usually takes 3-9 months to reduce the yeast to a level that causes no problem. Of course, this depends greatly on the degree of compliance to the program (both supplements and diet). After the yeast is under control, we usually do a 12 day D-tox Diet, one to four times a year (depending on diet and stress level) to keep it in check. The most important supplements which help lower yeast levels are Homeopathic Candida, vitamin C, beta-carotene, and *Acidophilus*-like organisms. We don't suggest adding the *Acidophilus*-like organisms until after at least a month and a half of weakening the yeast. Too hasty a use of these can often cause an "ecological battle" that is not all that comfortable. The most important thing is to maintain a good ecological balance of organisms in the body.

Single Herbs Pau d'arco, Garlic, Cardamon (the spice), Goldenseal root, Barberry, Coptis (Gold Thread), Ginger, Chamomile, Thyme, Melissa, Rosemary, Reishi, Shiitake.

Combinations Goldenseal Plus Formula, Reishi Extract, Stomach Formula, Lower Bowel Tonic (if constipated), Liver Formula (if sluggish liver); D-tox Diet (see Appendix).

Synergistic Vitamins and Minerals Beta-CEZB_6 (2 tablets, twice daily), Beta-carotene (30,000 IU, twice daily), B complex (25 mg, twice daily), Vitamin B_6 (50 mg daily), Vitamin C (2,000-5,000 mg daily), Acidophilus (1,000 mg, twice daily, rotating brands seem to have a better effect), Digestive Enzymes.

Suggested Program

Diet is the most important factor of all. Follow the diet in the appendix strictly. We usually start the program with a 12 day D-tox Diet.

Breakfast Candida 30X (5-10 drops), Beta-CEZB$_6$ (2 tablets), Digestive Enzymes (1-3 capsules, depending on size of meal), Acidophilus (1,000 mg, best on empty stomach, start after six weeks), Multivitamin/ mineral (1 tablet)
Snack Ester C (1,000 mg), Pau d'arco tea (1-2 cups)
Lunch Ester C (1,000 mg), Garlic (2 capsules), Candida 30X (5-10 drops)
Snack Ester C (1,000 mg) Herbal tea (1-2 cups of any above single herbs)
Supper same as breakfast, Garlic (2 capsules)
Evening Candida 30X (5-10 days)

Cankers

Cankers occur as sores in the mouth, either on the tongue, inside of the cheeks, on lip, or gums. They usually have a white center, surrounded by a red border. They can appear quickly but often leave just as quickly. They are often an indication of poor nutrition, or a chemical imbalance. They can be found more plentifully during festive seasons, or harvest times, when a person overconsumes a certain food like chocolate, tomatoes or oranges. They can be caused by a mild food allergy or sensitivity, stress, or poor gastrointestinal tract condition.

Recommended Action

If you are overconsuming a food, stop consuming it. Often a cleanse like the D-tox Diet (see Appendix) is indicated to help balance out body chemistry. A more alkaline diet, full of fresh vegetables, is almost always indicated. Sometimes cankers can be caused by rancid oils. By simply taking some non-rancid oil (especially Vitamin E or evening primrose oil) and applying it in the mouth, the canker will usually go away. If dietary changes don't affect the canker within a week, probably a hair analysis is indicated to see if there is a body chemistry imbalance.

Single Herbs Chlorella, Garlic, Goldenseal, Burdock, Red Clover, Pau D'arco, Dandelion, Evening Primrose Oil.

Combinations Goldenseal Plus Formula.

Synergistic Vitamins and Minerals Beta-CEZB_6 (2 tablets, twice daily), Ester C (2,000-5,000 mg daily), Vitamin E (400 IU), Zinc (15-50 mg daily), *Lactobacillus acidophilus*, L-lysine (500 mg, twice daily).

Cardiac Arrhythmias

See Heart.

Carpal Tunnel Syndrome (CTS)

This health issue is associated with tingling and/or burning pain in the first three fingers of the hand, particularly at night. It is caused by a swelling or thickening of the ligaments in the wrist. It is commonly associated with repetitive motion problems, injury, or bad office ergonomics. Carpal tunnel is most common in women (particularly those who are pregnant, on birth control pills or menopausal). This might be due to a higher need for Vitamin B_6 (pyridoxine) during these times.

Recommended Action

The most important supplement is Vitamin B_6. We usually use the Trauma Ointment, rubbed onto the area three to four times daily. It often is necessary to reduce Vitamin B_6 antagonists in the diet, such as yellow dye #5, hydralazine-treated food (such as potato chips), or excessive protein intake. After the initial stages of lowering inflammation we often get clients to use Chinese Bao-ding Balls for exercise.

Single Herbs Turmeric, Kava Kava.

Combinations Muscle Relaxing Formula.

Synergistic Vitamins and Minerals Beta-CEZB$_6$ (2 tablets, twice daily) Vitamin B$_6$ (50-250 mg, two to three times daily), Vitamin C (1,000 mg, twice daily), Bromelain (if CTS is from an injury, 250-500 mg between meals), Trauma Ointment.

Cataracts

See Eye Problems

Chronic Fatigue Syndrome

(See also Fibromyalgia, Candida)

Chronic Fatigue Syndrome (CFS) is known by many names. Some of the most common names are Myalgic Encephalomyelitis (ME), Chronic Fatigue and Immune Dysfunction Syndrome (CFIDS) and formerly known as Chronic Epstein-Barr Virus (CEBV). Whatever it is called, CFS is a psychoneuroimmunologic disorder, meaning it has aspects affecting the following three areas:

1. Psychology - affecting emotions and thinking of patient.
2. Neurology - chemically affecting the brain and nervous system.
3. Immunology - affecting the body's immune system.

There are a plethora of symptoms, (syndrome - a group of symptoms) but the most common ones are: chronic fatigue, insomnia, sore throat, muscle aches, joint inflammation, visual dysfunction, poor concentration or memory, anxiety and/or depression, headaches, fever, night sweats, hypersensitivity and allergies. These symptoms vary a great deal from person to person. Some people only having a few symptoms. CFS can occur in any age group and in both sexes, but anywhere from 65 - 80% are busy career women, depending on the study you read. It is very common among teachers, flight attendants, female lawyers and nurses.

Most of the people that we have seen (more than 800 patients) have above average constitutions, but have weakened their immune system. A workaholic lifestyle is seen in many patients, in others there is excessive aerobic exercise and in some, just stress.

I like to use a slightly altered model, developed originally by Dr. Jay Goldstein M.D., breaking CFS down into six phases. These phases are somewhat progressive but can often overlap:

1. Initial immunosuppression by agent "X" - this agent can be stress (environmental, or biological).
2. Initial viral infection or reinfection from resident viruses - with a weakened immune system, the body is left open to a viral onslaught.
3. Malfunction of immune system cytokine manufacturing/ functioning response - cytokine is the chemical that coordinates various parts of the immune system and communicates with the nervous system.
4. Abnormal generation of cytokines - miscommunication further disrupts immune and nervous systems.
5. Cytokines affect target organ receptors - various parts of the body (especially the brain and intestinal tract) start to malfunction due to faulty communications.
6. Malfunctioning of communication between organs - the body stops working as an integrated whole. Bidirectional transmission of information to and from organs and the immune system starts to malfunction.

It appears that the center of gravity of this health issue is in the limbic centers of the brain. This older part of the brain is responsible for some of the stress factors that trigger agent "x". The unknown agent could be a multitude of things, but it seems that stress is one of the most important ingredients.

Recommended Action

Our main objectives are to revitalize the body, build up the immune system, reduce any viruses or other opportunistic organisms in the body, restore proper internal communication, and reestablish normal sleep patterns. It is quite common to also have a yeast infection with CFS (refer to the Candida section). I have had many patients who immediately go out and start up aerobic exercise again when they begin to feel better. This seems to undo everything that is already accomplished so we suggest no aerobic type exercise for at least six months after a person feels better. Exercises like t'ai chi, seem to be quite good for CFS patients, when they feel like getting back into exercise. T'ai chi is an exercise that helps the body's energies communicate better, which is part of the intention of this Recommended Action.

Single Herbs Reishi, Echinacea, Astragalus, Licorice, Chlorella, Essential Fatty Acids.

Combinations Reishi Plus Formula, Shih Chuan Ta Pu Wan, Ener-Jazz, Echinacea Plus Formula.

Synergistic Vitamins and Minerals Beta-CEZB_6 (2-3 tablets, two to three times daily), Beta-carotene (20,000-50,000 IU, twice daily, B complex (1 tablet, twice daily), Vitamin C (2-6 grams daily), Zinc (15-60 mg daily).

Suggested Program

Breakfast Beta-CEZB_6 (2 tablets), Reishi Plus Formula (3 capsules), Chlorella (1,500 mg), Shih Chuan Ta Pu Wan (8 tablets), Echinacea (2 capsules).
Snack Ester C (500 mg), Ener-Jazz (1 tsp).
Lunch Shih Chuan Ta Pu Wan (8 tablets), Ester C (500 mg).
Snack Same as morning
Supper Same as breakfast
Bedtime Valerian Plus Formula (2-3 capsules).

Coeliac disease

(Also consider Candida)

This rather rare health problem is the result of an allergy to gluten. If the person does not show symptoms by their tenth year, consider Candida, irritable bowel syndrome or other intestinal problems as a related or underlying cause. The symptoms include nausea, diarrhea, abdominal bloating, foul-smelling stools, weight loss, anaemia, skin rashes and joint and/or bone pain.

Recommended Action

If a person is truly a coeliac, they have to avoid wheat, barley and oats. Sometimes other grains have to be avoided at least initially. It is usually important to avoid most dairy products. Usually butter and yogurt are alright to consume. Response is relatively quick. More than 80% have noticeable changes within the first month. If no response is seen within this period of time, there might be other associated problems.

Often after 2-6 months of being on the diet, occasional consumption (1-2 times a week) of the restricted food is possible. If Candida is involved, the whole Candida program should be followed.

Single Herbs Alfalfa, Chlorella, Goldenseal, Barberry.

Combinations Goldenseal Plus Formula, Huang Lian Su.

Synergistic Vitamins and Minerals Beta-CEZB$_6$ (2 tablets, twice daily), Beta-carotene (20,000 IU, twice daily), Vitamin C (1,000 mg, twice daily), Vitamin E (400 IU daily), Multiple vitamin/mineral, Zinc (25-50 mg).

Colds and Flus

We all know the various symptom related to colds and flus too well. They include various combinations of the following: head congestion, sore throat, difficulty breathing, coughing, headaches, fever, restlessness, sneezing, watery eyes, stomach aches, diarrhea, ache and pains. If a fever gets above 102°F, you should consult a health practitioner. These health issues are hard to cure if they get into their advanced stages, so prevention, or proper care in the first stage, is the best bet. Factors that can compromise the immune system include: too much sugar, chronic overeating, too much mucus-forming foods, toxic bowels, Candida, food sensitivities (especially dairy and flour). Stress can also be a contributing factor.

Long term use of Echinacea

Many people in the health food industry feel that you cannot take Echinacea on an ongoing basis. It is felt that it will lose it potency after 10-20 days. It has been shown that the original source of this concept was a mistranslation of a German paper. Many practitioners have been using echinacea clinically on an ongoing basis without noting a reduction in function. Putting it in a formula with other herbs seems to ensure that it will work best for long-term use.

Recommended Action

The cure for colds and flus is prevention. The best prevention is to protect the immune system by eating well, getting adequate exercise (not overdoing it), fresh air, clean water and preventive herbs. One of the best herbs for flu prevention is echinacea. We find the echinacea root works best as a prophylactic in powder (capsule or tablet) form. At the first stage of a cold, echinacea is best in a tincture form, especially if mixed with goldenseal root. Vitamin C is also a great prophylactic. Once a person is 3-5 days into a cold/flu, neither of them will stop the problem.

What to use

Single Herbs Echinacea, Goldenseal root, Licorice, Garlic, Ginger, Astragalus, Lomatium, Elder Berries, Yarrow, Mints, Eucalyptus oil.

Combinations Echinacea Plus Formula, Goldenseal Plus Formula, Echinacea/Goldenseal tincture, Kam Wo tea.

Synergistic Vitamins and Minerals Beta-CEZB$_6$ (2-3 tablets, 2-3 times daily), Beta-carotene (30,000 IU, 3 times daily), Vitamin C (5,000-10,000 mg), Zinc (30-60 mg).

Suggested Program

Prevention Beta-CEZB$_6$ (2 tablets, twice daily), Echinacea Plus Formula (2-3 tablets, two-three times daily), Ester C (1,000 mg, twice daily), Ginger root tea (1-2 cups daily).

First stage Beta-CEZB$_6$ (3 tablets, three times daily), Ester C (1,000 mg, every two hours), Garlic (2 capsules every three hours), Ginger root tea (2-6 cups daily), Echinacea/Goldenseal Tincture (1 tsp every two hours). Drink lots of hot liquids

Colitis

Colitis is an inflammation of the colon (large intestine). It may be simply a mucus condition or it may be ulcerative, with blood as well as mucus showing up in the stool. Diarrhea is common, sometimes alternating with constipation. Loss of weight, anemia, and even toxemia are common complications. Others symptoms include hemorrhoids, abscesses, and prolapse of the colon. Depression and other emotional conditions can precipitate attacks of colitis.

Recommended Action

Limit the diet to juices or pureed fruits and vegetables. Lots of steam-distilled or reverse osmosis water is beneficial, along with the following.

Combinations Psyllax (soothe colon, aid in ulceration, slow down diarrhea); Lower Bowel Tonic (to tone and strengthen colon); Cleansing Formula, Goldenseal Plus Formula, Huang Lian su.

Synergistic Vitamins and Minerals Vitamin A (20,000 to 40,000 IU); B complex (1 tablet, twice daily); Calcium/Magnesium (2 twice daily); Vitamin C (500 mg, twice daily).

Suggested Program

Start with three Huang Lian Su (Berberini HCl) or Goldenseal Plus Formula three times daily, one tablespoon of Psyllax in one cup of tomato juice twice daily (if tomato juice irritates, use other liquid). After one week take one Lower Bowel Tonic daily, increase to one tablet, two times daily after one more week. In third week add one Cleansing Formula. In the fourth week add one more Cleansing Formula. By the fourth week you should be taking: 1 Lower Bowel Tonic (twice daily), 1 Cleansing Formula (twice daily), 1 tablespoon of Psyllax (twice daily) and 3 Huang Lian Su (three times daily).

Constipation

See Bowel and Colon.

Coughs

Coughing is an attempt by the body to dislodge and expel some irritating or obstructing matter from the chest or throat and consists of reflex action of the respiratory muscles accompanied by a blast of air. Demulcent and expectorant herbs help to loosen and break up the offending substance (if it is mucus), so it can then be expelled. Even the most bothersome cough can be helped by drinking a little warm water mixed with one tablespoon of lemon juice and one tablespoon of honey. Antispasmodic herbs are necessary to treat spasmodic coughs since this kind involves irritation of a nerve which then activates the coughing reflex.

Single Herbs Ma Huang, Gumweed, Licorice root, Slippery Elm (lozenges), Marshmallow, Mullein, Comfrey (demulcents and expectorants); Lobelia Extract (antispasmodic and expectorant)

Combinations Lung Formula.

Synergistic Vitamins and Minerals Beta-CEZB$_6$, Vitamin A (20,000 - 50,000 IU), Vitamin B Complex (25-50 mg), Vitamin C (3000 - 5000 mg), Calcium (20 mg).

Two Chinese cough syrups of note are African Sea Coconut and Pie Pa Koa. Sea coconut is excellent with most colds and coughs. Pie Pa Koa is excellent for dry coughs but not when mucus is running.

When and when not to suppress a cough

Some coughs should be suppressed and some shouldn't. If a cough is full of mucus, we want to encourage the expectoration of the mucus. But if the cough is a dry cough, there is usually some sort of irritation in the throat. With a dry cough try to soothe the throat and thereby stop the cough. Also consider if a throat problem might be caused by drainage from the sinuses. Honey is good to moisten dry mucus. If a dry cough, hot honey (1 tbsp.) in a glass of hot lemon and water will often loosen up mucus. Don't use honey if mucus is already runny.

Cramps

Cramps may indicate a mineral imbalance and particularly a deficiency of calcium or magnesium. They consist of spasmodic, involuntary muscle contractions which are generally accompanied by great pain.

Single Herbs Alfalfa, Cayenne or Cayenne Extract (leg and muscle cramps); Ginger (uterine); Chamomile, Peppermint (stomach); Kava Kava, Lobelia Extract, Cramp Bark (antispasmodic).

Combinations Muscle Relaxing Formula (leg and muscle cramps); Female Formula (Uterine cramps); Stomach Formula (stomach), Lower Bowel Tonic (intestinal).

Synergistic Vitamins and Minerals Vitamin D (400 IU), Vitamin B$_6$ (50-100 mg), Pantothenic Acid (100 mg), Calcium citrate (600-1500 mg), Magnesium Oxide (300-800 mg), Vitamin E (400-1000 IU), Magnesium Phosphate 6-12X tissue salt (four when needed), Multiminerals, and trace minerals.

Suggested Program

If the cramps are intestinal or uterine take a few capsules of ginger, or a tea of equal parts of ginger, Blessed Thistle and Cramp Bark. If the cramps are in a large muscle take plenty of calcium, magnesium, and Magnesium Phosphate tissue salts, and three Muscle Relaxing Formula, three times daily. Cayenne and Arnica Tincture applied to the area will help ease cramps and stimulate circulation. B and B Tincture, taken orally or mixed into a liniment, is beneficial.

Crohn's disease

see also Colitis

Crohn's is a chronic long term inflammation of all levels of the intestinal wall. It is characterized by diarrhea, cramping, fever, malabsorption and loss of energy. We normally do the same therapy for Crohn's as outlined for colitis.

We also usually add the herbal tincture Ener-Jazz (1-2 tsp., 2-6 times daily).

Cysts

see also Breast Problems

Cysts usually appear just under the surface of the skin and are abnormal sac-like growths which contain fluid or semi-fluid substance. They are also common on the mucous membranes of the body, particularly those of the female reproductive organs. They are distinguishable from tumors, which consist of solid matter, in that they contain mucus, dead tissue debris, pus or even hair, but they are rarely malignant.

Recommended Action

While you are trying to eliminate cysts, the Cleansing Diet should be followed for ten days, alternating with the Daily Diet Regime. It is often beneficial to add in the third cycle of a three-day Cleansing fast (see Appendix). Then repeat the cycle. Whole grains are also very beneficial to rid the body of cysts.

Single Herbs Black Walnut leaves, hulls, bark, or Extract; Burdock, Chaparral, Evening Primrose Oil or other essential fatty acid oils.

Combinations Female Formula (cysts in female areas); Chlorella, Goldenseal Plus Formula (cysts anywhere).

Depression

Two different approaches that have worked with depression

The most important supplement for depression is a homeopathic/Bach Flower combination: Aurum 30/ Gorse 30X.

Since depression is often a case of pent-up energies, some form of creative expression helps to release and rechannel energy. I have often seen people write their way out of depression. Just sitting and writing (without a concern for perfection) can be a great therapy.

Depression is a chronic emotional state that a person might, or might not, admit to. It usually has the symptoms of fatigue, insomnia (sometimes hypersomnia), loss of appetite (sometimes ravenous appetite), physical inactivity (sometimes hyperactivity), headaches, backaches and a feeling of worthlessness, diminished ability to think or concentrate, and often thoughts of death and suicide. There can be many factors that cause depression such as a loss in the family, loss of a job, etc. Usually, time will help to overcome these types of depression. Other factors such as nutritional deficiencies, food and/or airborne allergies, hypoglycemia, Candida, low thyroid function, heavy mineral toxicity, endometriosis or seasonal affective disorder could be the underlying cause.

Often a depressed person does need counselling, but depression can often be overcome by supplementation, without the use of antidepressant drugs. Sometimes, short use of an antidepressant drug is needed to help get the person back on track (i.e., for the nutritional supplements to have time to function properly).

Recommended Action

The first and most important thing is to determine if there are any underlying problems such as Candida, allergies, etc. It is significant to have a whole food diet, reducing sugars, caffeine, alcohol and altered oils (e.g., rancid oil, margarine, etc.). Eat a significant amount of complex carbohydrates, such as brown rice, millet and buckwheat. Soybeans and soybean products (like tofu) are often beneficial as are raw fruits and vegetables. Regular exercise, without being too strenuous, is very helpful.

Single Herbs Reishi, St. John's Wort, Ginkgo, Essential Fatty Acids.

Combinations Reishi Plus Formula, St. John's Wort Extract Plus Formula, Ginkgo Plus Formula.

Synergistic Vitamins and Minerals Beta-CEZB_6 (2 tablets, twice daily), B complex (1 tablet, twice daily), Vitamin B_6 (50 mg, three times daily), Folic acid (400 mcg daily), Vitamin B_{12} (250-1,000 mcg, daily), Vitamin C (1,000 mg, three times daily), Phosphatylcholine (2,400 mg, twice daily), Magnesium (500mg daily).

Suggested Program

Pre-breakfast Aurum/Gorse 30X* (5-10 drops)
Breakfast Reishi Plus Formula (3 capsules), Beta-CEZB_6 (2 tablets), B complex (1 tablet, with folic acid and Vitamin B_{12}), St. John's Wort Extract Plus Formula(2 capsules), Phosphatylcholine (2,400 mg).
Snack Aurum/Gorse 30X (5-10 drops)
Lunch St. John's Wort Extract Plus Formula (2 capsules)
Snack Aurum/Gorse 30X (5-10 drops)
Supper same as Breakfast.

* Aurum/Gorse can be taken as needed. There is no toxicity. If a person is having a rough time, it can be taken up to every 15 minutes.

Diabetes

See Pancreas.

Diaper Rash

Diaper rash, otherwise known as diaper dermatitis, is a localized skin irritation. It is caused by extensive skin contact with a wet or soiled diaper and can range in severity from mild redness to blistering. It is commonly followed by secondary yeast or bacterial infections.

Recommended Action

Changing the diapers more frequently will avoid further irritation. The skin should be kept clean and dry with air circulating to it as much as possible. Avoid the use of plastic pants. Chickweed or Mullein ointment should be applied to give relief.

Single Herbs Mullein (topically applied); Oil of Garlic (topically applied). Black Walnut Extract (topically applied, especially for yeast infections); Chickweed ointment (emollient); Chamomile tea (wash), Zinc Oxide ointment.

A Mullein Diaper

Dr. J. R. Christopher tells a story of a very poor woman who couldn't afford proper diapers for her child, and diaper rash was the result. Things got financially worse for the lady so she tried to make diapers out of some big mullein leaves, and to her astonishment the child's diaper rash went away. Both mullein and chickweed ointments are excellent for diaper rash.

Diarrhea

Frequent and abnormal liquid bowel movements are indications of this condition. Other body disorders such as colitis, amoebic dysentery, food or chemical poisoning and emotional stress can cause diarrhea. It can also be brought on by infection (either in the digestive tract or elsewhere in the body) or by digestive problems resulting from chemical, hormonal or enzyme deficiencies, or it may occur by itself. If the diet has just been changed to one high in roughage, or fiber, and fresh fruits, diarrhea will often result until the body adjusts. Dehydration, loss of minerals, and loss of water-soluble vitamins and beneficial intestinal flora (bacteria) will occur if the condition is not remedied.

Recommended Action

Diarrhea should be treated as a symptom and efforts should be made to determine the cause. It is advisable to replace lost fluid by drinking large quantities of juice or some other liquid. Astringent herbs can be employed both orally and in the form of an enema. If the diarrhea is a result of amoebic dysentery, colitis, emotional stress, food poisoning or any other disorder, it is important to deal with that particular condition specifically. In cases of extreme constipation, nothing but water can get through and this condition manifests itself as diarrhea. The obstruction can be removed by the use of an enema, and the peristaltic muscles can be stimulated and gradually rebuilt by the use of appropriate herbs. If there is excessive bleeding of the bowel, make a tea from one ounce mullein leaves simmered in one pint of milk. Strain and drink it immediately after the bowels move. This is an effective remedy and will often achieve results where all else fails. The mullein acts as a homeostatic and demulcent and is held against the membrane walls by the milk which coats them. Make a fresh batch each

Stop diarrhea

The Chinese supplement Huang Lian Su or Berberini HCl is a concentrated extract of *Coptis chinensis*. It is very good for stopping diarrhea. Take 3 tablets, three times daily. *Coptis* can also be found in the Goldenseal Plus Formula.

time and drink the whole thing immediately after each bowel movement until the bleeding stops. In infantile diarrhea the loss of potassium can be serious or even fatal. Mashed banana will supply a large amount of potassium and halt the diarrhea.

Single Herbs White Oak bark, Red Raspberry (astringent enema); Slippery Elm, Huang Lian Su (astringent and demulcent); Mullein (for bleeding bowel); Fluid Extract of Wild Strawberry, Uva Ursi (astringent).

Combinations Curing pills, Huang Lian Su or Goldenseal Plus Formula, Psyllax.

Suggested Program

Breakfast Curing Pills (1-2 vials with a hot liquid), Huang Lian Su (2-3 tablets), Psyllax (1 tbsp.), Goldenseal Plus Formula (2 capsules).

Lunch same as breakfast

Supper same as breakfast

Digestion

Digestion is a process of breaking down the foods we eat and changing them into a form which is easily assimilated by the body's cells to use for energy, tissue replacement and growth. The digestive process begins in the mouth. All food should be thoroughly chewed to break fibers and other hard matter apart. Chewing is also important to ensure that the first of the digestive enzymes found in the saliva are properly mixed in with the food. The next stage of digestion takes place in the stomach, where more enzymes are added along with HCl. Only alcohol, water, some Vitamin C and certain sugars are absorbed in the stomach. The food moves on to the small intestine where additional enzymes are secreted, from both the pancreas and the small intestine itself. Here, bile which comes from the liver, is also added and acts as an alkalizer and laxative and assists in the breakdown of fats. Most of the absorption of nutrients takes place in the small intestine. The nutrients are then carried by the blood to the cells. The waste products of digestion are passed along to the large intestine, where some minerals and water are reabsorbed and finally the waste is excreted. In this long chain of events, we often see many symptomatic problems manifested. These can include heartburn, gas, acid indigestion, constipation, diarrhea, vomiting, colic and other conditions (treated individually under the particular heading for that problem). The digestive system must be functioning properly if we are to get the healthy nutrients we need into our bodies. Otherwise it is possible to starve in the midst of plenty while the much-needed vitamins and herbs are flushed away.

Poor Digestion

Probably 80% of the people that come into my clinic have some sort of digestive problem. The most common is the lack of proper enzymes and gastric juice production. This is often caused by simply eating too fast for many years, resulting first in low hydrochloric acid production in the stomach. Giving the person Stomach Formula will usually build up the stomach in three to nine months, at which time we can stop its usage. In most cases we start with some Digestive Enzymes during the meal.

Recommended Action

Overeating, eating in a rushed or excited (stress) state, improper mastication (chewing) and salivation, and poor food combinations (eating the wrong foods together) are the most common causes of digestive problems. The solutions are obviously simple: never overeat, eat moderate amounts and only when hungry. Take the time to eat in a relaxed state. Avoid eating if you are rushed or emotionally upset. Chew each mouthful slowly and thoroughly, and avoid "inhaling" food. Finally, foods such as refined starches and sugars contribute to poor digestion and putrefaction, resulting in gas and other improper acid balances in the stomach, and so should be avoided. To help correct the acid balance in the stomach (whether too high or too low) take 1 tablespoon of apple cider vinegar in a glass of warm water sweetened with 1 teaspoon honey, before meals. Fermented foods such as yogurt, miso and sauerkraut can aid digestion and help prevent intestinal putrefaction. Garlic and bee pollen are also beneficial in preventing putrefaction and will help eliminate gas. Herbs of a stomachic, bitter and aromatic nature will aid digestion, while those that are carminative will eliminate gas, and herbs such as comfrey, which is demulcent in nature, will soothe the mucous membranes of the digestive tract.

Single Herbs Catnip, Chamomile, Ginger (aromatic); Cayenne, Ginseng, Peppermint (stomachic); Fennel, Fenugreek, Wild Yam (carminative); Saffron, Meadowsweet (antacid); Papaya Leaves (digestive enzyme), Garlic, Bee Pollen, Comfrey, Chlorella.

Combinations Stomach Formula, Digestive Enzymes, Reishi Plus Formula, Goldenseal Plus Formula.

Synergistic Vitamins and Minerals B complex, Digestive Enzymes.

Suggested Program

Although long term use can become habit-forming, starting off with Digestive Enzymes specific to the problem, (usually one-four with the major meals) can add to a herbal program. The enzymes will help to digest the herbs more fully so the rest of the digestive system can gradually take over with its own enzymes, allowing the elimination of those taken orally. This process usually takes about two-six months. Working with the digestion is often the best place to start a general herbal building program. Take two Stomach Formula before two meals daily, one - two Lower Bowel Tonic (if slow-moving bowels) twice daily from the start of the program.

Diverticulitis

Diverticulitis occurs when diverticula (small pouch-like sacs found in mucous membranes, particularly those of the large intestine) become inflamed. These pouches are abnormal but pose no real health problem by themselves. However, if food particles become entrapped in them, which is a common occurrence, inflammation will result. It is usually accompanied by fever, constipation, severe abdominal pain and occasionally blood in the stool. It is possible for the intestinal passage to become partially blocked in some cases.

Recommended Action

See treatment for colitis.

Synergistic Vitamins and Minerals Folic acid (one mg daily), Multiminerals and vitamins (two daily), Garlic oil capsules, Whey powder (one tablespoon with each meal), Cod Liver oil (two tablespoons daily).

Dizziness

Dizziness is characterized by feelings of giddiness, unsteadiness, lightheadedness or faintness. In some cases it is a normal reaction to a change in atmosphere, such as the reduced amount of oxygen at higher altitudes. It can also indicate constipation, menstrual problems, high or low blood pressure, hypoglycemia, anemia, diabetes, arteriosclerosis or temporary lack of circulation to the brain. Vertigo is the medical term for the sensation of spinning or falling, or of standing still while the surrounding objects seem to be moving. Often it goes hand in hand with nausea, vomiting, perspiration and headache. It invariably originates in the inner ear, the body's equilibrium center (sense of balance). Occasionally brain tumors are responsible for the problem, but more often it is a result of an ear infection or head injury.

Recommended Action

It is first necessary to determine if dizziness is merely a symptom of another problem in order to find and rectify the cause. In a multitude of situations simple constipation is the cause, especially if headaches are also present and relief from the dizzy sensation can be obtained by the use of stimulant herbs. In a true case of vertigo, the cause must again be determined and steps taken to relieve any accompanying nausea and vomiting. Nervine herbs can help to restore function of the inner ear. Every night before retiring put a few drops of garlic oil in each ear; follow this with a few drops of ear and nerve drops (B and B Tincture). A three-day cleansing fast or D-Tox can also be helpful.

Single Herbs Ginkgo, Cayenne, Peppermint, Dandelion root (for relief of dizziness).

Combinations B and B Tincture, Nerve Formula.

Synergistic Vitamins and Minerals B complex (50 mg ratio, two times daily), Vitamin B_6 (150 mg, two times daily), Vitamin C (1,000 mg daily).

Earaches And Ear Infections

These problems are extremely common especially in young children. They will often indicate the presence of a problem by pulling or rubbing their ears if they are unable to speak. Earaches are often a symptom of a number of other conditions such as head injuries, infection of the eyes, ears, nose, throat or glandular system. Several home remedies are available to relieve the pain. If the pain is caused by infection, the source should be determined. Injury, intrusion of foreign matter, or such things as swimming in contaminated water usually cause outer ear infections (from the eardrum outward). Infections which spread from the nose and throat through the eustachian tubes usually cause middle ear infections (the small cavity on the inside of the eardrum). This type often involves diminished hearing and a feeling of fullness in the ear along with pain and fever. It is inner ear infections which upset the body's equilibrium center causing dizziness, nausea, vomiting and partial or total loss of hearing. This is often the result of a spreading middle ear infection (otitis media) or meningitis.

Recommended Action

The most common cause of ear infection is an allergy to dairy and sometime flour. Often by following a low mucus diet long term relief can be found. Immediate relief from the pain of earache can be obtained by placing ice packs on the affected ear. Always treat both ears when dealing with infection; this will keep the infection from spreading from one ear to the other. To relieve pain and drain out infection, lightly bake an onion cut in half; take the warm onion and place half over each ear and hold in place overnight with a large wrapped bandage, or use a herbal fomentation. Middle and inner ear problems are helped by the insertion of a few drops of garlic oil in each ear. Herbs which fight infection should also be taken orally.

Single Herbs Chamomile, Hops, Mullein (oil as drops or for fomentations over the ears); Oil of Garlic, Lobelia Extract (ear drops); Goldenseal (infection).

Combinations Goldenseal Plus Formula, three parts Mullein and one part Lobelia used as an external fomentation. B and B Tincture (3 drops) followed by Garlic oil (3 drops) in ear for six nights, on the seventh night rinse ear with equal parts apple cider vinegar and water using an ear syringe.

Synergistic Vitamins and Minerals Beta-CEZB_6, Vitamin A (20,000 IU daily); Vitamin C (2,000 mg daily); Calcium/Magnesium (two, twice daily).

Suggested Program

Breakfast Goldenseal Plus Formula (2-3 capsules), Beta-CEZB$_6$ (2 tablets).
Snack Ester C (500 mg)
Lunch Multivitamins (or Children's multiple)(1 tablet)
Snack as morning
Supper same as breakfast

Eczema

(See Skin)

Edema

Edema (dropsy, water retention) is an abnormal accumulation of fluid in the body tissues. Because the blood is moving slowly, it accumulates and exerts an outward pressure on the walls of the vein. When this pressure becomes greater than the inward osmotic pressure, fluids from the blood escape into the intercellular spaces and cause the characteristic swelling of legs, hands, etc. Pulmonary edema (cardiac dropsy) is caused by failure of the heart to pump blood from the lungs at an adequate rate. This causes pressure in the pulmonary veins, forcing fluid into the lungs. In kidney-related edema, severe loss of blood plasma protein in the urine causes the reverse osmotic pressure and subsequent water retention.

Recommended Action

The solution to all these forms of edema lies in the kidneys and lymphatic system. Most of the excess fluid can be eliminated through the kidneys with the assistance of diuretic herbs and a glandular cleanser. Vapor baths and diaphoretics will also help eliminate a significant portion through the skin. Apply diuretics and diaphoretics as fomentations over affected areas and take them orally also to achieve relief. Avoid salt, meats, pastries, etc. in the diet.

Single Herbs Parsley, Juniper berries, Gravel root (diuretics).

Combinations Kidney/Bladder Formula, Parsley/Raspberry leaf tea (1 tsp. of each in 1 cup boiled water); 3 parts Mullein to one part Lobelia (as tea and fomentation).

Synergistic Vitamins and Minerals B complex (25 mg), Vitamin B_6 (50 - 200 mg); Vitamin C (2,000 - 5,000 mg), Potassium Gluconate, Bromelain (pineapple enzyme).

Suggested Program

A juice fast for 3-10 days is very beneficial for this if not contraindicated by other health issues. The best juices include cucumber, pineapple and watermelon (or the Lemon Aid Cleanse). (The fast should include only one of the above). Lymphatic drainage massages, done by a professional, are very beneficial as are rebounders (small trampolines) when used for fifteen minutes daily. Take two Kidney/Bladder Formula three times daily along with parsley and red raspberry leaf tea and mullein and lobelia tea daily. We often add Nat. Mur, Nat. Sulph. which are tissue salts. If a fast is not feasible, do 24 days of the D-Tox Diet.

Eye Problems

There are many eye problems. Most people have experienced at least one from time to time. Bloodshot, burning, dry, infected, irritated, sensitive to light, watery ... the descriptive list for common eye issues is lengthy. Many of these problems are related to stress or allergies. Watery eyes can often accompany a cold/flu. Protruding eyes are usually associated with thyroid problems. Yellow "whites" of the eye represent jaundice and indicate problems in the liver/gallbladder area. Dark circles under the eyes represent allergies, but might also indicate problems in the kidneys/adrenal area.

Cataracts occur when the lenses of the eye become clouded or opaque, making it hard to focus on close and distant objects. The problem is progressive, continuing into loss of vision. Many factors can contribute to cataracts including ocular disease, injury, side effects of pharmaceuticals, surgery, systemic diseases (e.g., diabetes), toxins, ultraviolet light, diet. Cataracts are the number one cause of blindness.

Recommended Action

For general eye health, a good whole diet is necessary. A diet high in broccoli, cabbage, carrots, cauliflower, green vegetables, squash, sunflower seeds and watercress is best. Whole grains are very good for the eyes, while white flour is not. Dairy and sugar should also be kept to a minimum. Carrot juice and/or cod liver oil is excellent for eye health. Essential fatty acids (EFAs) are very important to keep the eyes from drying out. Cold water fish and flax seed oil are ideal sources of EFAs. Shellfish are not advised when a person has continuous dry eye problems. Often wearing glasses with UV protection (especially while in the sun) will help prevent certain problems like cataracts.

Single Herbs Eyebright, Goldenseal root, Essential Fatty Acids (Evening Primrose oil, Borage oil etc.), Bayberry (astringent), Raspberry leaves, Chamomile (soothing),

Combinations Goldenseal Plus Formula, Hachimijiogan (Chinese herbal formula).

Synergistic Vitamins and Minerals Beta-CEZB$_6$ (2 tablets, twice daily), Beta-carotene (100,000 IU, twice daily), B complex (1 tablet, twice daily), Vitamin C (1,000 mg, three times daily), Vitamin E (400-800 IU daily), Selenium (400 mcg daily), Zinc (15-60 mg daily), Copper (3 mg daily), L-cysteine (400 mg daily), L-glutamine (200 mg daily), L-glycine (200 mg daily).

Fatigue

see also Chronic Fatigue Syndrome

This is a feeling of mental or physical tiredness which may be the result of physical exertion, mental or emotional stress, rapid weight loss or boredom. On the other hand, it is possible that fatigue is a symptom of anemia, hypoglycemia, nutritional deficiency, obesity or acute infectious disease. Headache, backache, indigestion or general irritability may often accompany fatigue. Cross reference should be made to the above subjects if any of these are suspected.

Recommended Action

The specific underlying disorder must be discovered and dealt with before long term relief can be obtained. A period of rest should follow exercise, perhaps a much needed change will relieve boredom, while detoxification and nutritional supplementation may help in cases of rapid weight loss.

Single Herb Siberian Ginseng, Chinese Ginseng, Gotu Kola, Fo-ti-teng, Cat's Claw.

Synergistic Vitamins and Minerals B complex, Multivitamins and minerals, Multiminerals, Digestive Enzymes.

Combinations Ener-Jazz, Shih Chuan Ta Pu Wan, Four Ginsengs.

Suggested Program

Breakfast Digestive Enzymes (1-3 capsules), Four Ginsengs (2 capsules), Multivitamins and minerals (1 tablet).
Snack Ener-Jazz (1 tsp.)
Lunch same as breakfast
Snack Ener-Jazz (1 tsp.)
Supper Digestive Enzymes (1-3 capsules), Multivitamins and minerals (1 tablet)
Consider doing a 12 day D-Tox Diet.

Fevers

Fever can be brought on by a number of causes but is usually related to bacterial or viral infections. Invading microorganisms and the toxins they release, combined with an excessive accumulation of toxic wastes, upset the body's temperature control mechanism in the hypothalamus (located centrally at the base of the brain), causing abnormally high body temperatures. Natural healers suggest that these "germs" are rather like little garbage men which feed on and dispose of the accumulated toxic material. Once these wastes are cleaned up, the bacteria begin to die of starvation and are eliminated from the body through discharges and excretions. The fever then breaks and the body enters the recovery stage.

Recommended Action

Usually it is best to encourage and assist a fever, unless it becomes excessively high (about 103° F.). In this case use febrifuges such as yarrow, Blessed Thistle, chamomile, fenugreek, lobelia or thyme. Take plenty of fluids when in a fever. Consider the example of a desert and a jungle: it is apparent that dry heat does not support much life, while moist heat germinates and gives life. Often if the diet is restricted to liquids and the bowels are relieved as soon as a fever is apparent, the fever will break. This in itself can turn into a fairly thorough cleansing. So, a fever can often be a blessing in disguise. It is always advisable to ingest large quantities of liquid. A good tea is chamomile.

If the fever does not subside take the following steps: Use a herbal enema of catnip, sage or Red raspberry tea to help the bowels move if constipation is present. After the bowel is cleaned, use pressed or finely grated garlic in one-half pint of distilled water and one-half pint of apple cider vinegar taken as a rectal enema. Follow this with a hot bath to which one ounce each of cayenne, ginger, and dry mustard have been added. This will stimulate the system and promote perspiration. To assist the fever and allay thirst, take warm (never cold) diaphoretic teas such as yarrow, catnip, chamomile, Blessed Thistle or sage while in the bath. To prevent fainting while in the bath, place a cold towel or washcloth on the forehead. Immediately upon stepping out of the bath, wrap a large double cotton white sheet (soaked in cold water) around the body and pin it so that only the head and feet can be seen. Next, put the individual in bed, still in the sheet and cover well with wool blankets. Oil the feet well all the way up to the ankles with olive oil then apply a paste of grated garlic and Vaseline (half and half) to the soles of the feet only. Use a length of gauze bandage to cover the sole of the foot where the paste is and use a large sock to hold everything in place. Finally pin the bottom of the cold wet sheet closed to form a sack. In the morning the fever will have broken. The sheet will have dried from the heat of the fever and will often be stained by toxic waste that was eliminated with the perspiration.

Single Herbs Yarrow, Blessed Thistle, Black Walnut, Chamomile, Fenugreek, Raspberry (Diaphoretics), Wormwood.

No Vitamins or Minerals should be taken during fever.
Refer to Daily Food Regime after the fever has broken, for a building program.

Fibrocystic Breast

See Breast Problems

Fibromyalgia

see also Chronic Fatigue Syndrome

Considered by many to be a subcategory of Chronic Fatigue Syndrome (CFS), fibromyalgia (FM), is characterized by widespread musculoskeletal pain with a set of specific tender points. It is usually associated with fatigue and sleep disturbance. Several other symptoms that might be present are: irritability, poor memory and concentration, headaches, dizziness and bowel complaints. Women are afflicted with FM ten times more often than men, with the normal age group between twenty and fifty-five.

Recommended Action

This health issue, like many others, is classified as a psychoneuroimmunological syndrome. This means that it has psychological, neurological and immunological aspects. The center of gravity of the syndrome varies from person to person and from time to time within an individual.

Counselling is just as important with this syndrome as any form of supplementation. Typically a FM person has a very good constitution while simultaneously being very sensitive to their environment. This sensitivity extends to both interpersonal issues and toxins in the environment. FM people often internalize a large amount of emotional and mental data, creating circular arguments in their mind. This circular argument mental pattern seems to tighten up muscle tissue, creating a stagnation of both fluid and what the Chinese call *qi* (chee). The best supplement we have found for relaxing this internalization of circular arguments is reishi.

It is also important to strengthen the immune system with good diet, mild exercise (e.g. t'ai chi or stretching) and clean air, along with supplementation. Low levels of magnesium and malic acid can often be found in FM people.

Ms C and FM

Ms C, was 29 years old when she came in with fibromyalgia. She had all the sore points, and carpal tunnel syndrome. She had well above average intelligence and was extremely sensitive. She felt that she was responsible for everything that happened in her family and was very concerned over her parents' health, who live thousands of miles away. You could almost see her muscles tighten up in response to things. After following a program similar to the one listed, plus doing t'ai chi, she was back in good health within 3 months. She followed this up with counselling to release her excessive sense of responsibility for others. The average FM program takes 3-9 months.

Single Herbs Reishi, Chlorella, St. John's Wort, Ginkgo.

Combinations Reishi Plus Formula, St. John's Wort Extract Plus Formula, Inflammation Ointment.

Synergistic Vitamins and Minerals Beta-CEZB$_6$ (2 tablets, twice daily), Beta-carotene (30,000 IU, twice daily), B complex (1 tablet, twice daily), Vitamin C (1,000 mg, four times daily), Magnesium (300-600 mg daily), Malic acid (1,200-2,400 mg daily).

Suggested Program

Pre-breakfast apply Inflammation Ointment

Breakfast Reishi Plus Formula (3 capsules), Chlorella (1,500 mg), St. John's Wort Extract Plus Formula (2 capsules), Beta-CEZB$_6$ (2 tablets), Malic acid (600-1,200 mg), Magnesium (150-300 mg), B complex (1 tablet).

Snack apply Inflammation Ointment, Ester C (1,000 mg)

Lunch Reishi Plus Formula (2 capsules)

Snack same as morning

Supper Same as Breakfast

Evening apply Inflammation Ointment, Ester C (1,000 mg)

Food Poisoning

Certain bacteria such as staphylococcus, streptococcus, salmonella, shigella and the clostridium bacteria are responsible for food poisoning. The contamination generally is a result of improper food handling and preparation. Using aluminum or unglazed ceramic earthenware for cooking can also cause symptoms like food poisoning and so should be avoided at all costs.

Recommended Action

Use an emetic to empty the stomach of its contaminated contents so that they will not be further assimilated into the system. Salt water is commonly used, but a large dose (1 tsp. - 1 tbsp.) of lobelia is unsurpassed for results. Follow this treatment with a quantity of juice and/or distilled water to dilute the toxins that were already absorbed by the system. It is best to follow food poisonings with one day of juice fast, followed by five days of Inner Cleanse diet (refer to Appendix).

Single Herbs Lobelia (emetics).

Fractures

Injury, rather than disease, is the usual cause of broken bones or fractures.

Recommended Action

Follow the usual first aid procedures: make sure breathing is unobstructed, guard against shock, control bleeding by the application of direct pressure when necessary, and prevent unnecessary movement of the fractured part. Knitting and healing will take place more readily if the following herbal aids are used after the bone has been set.

Single Herbs Comfrey, Aloe Vera.

Combinations Vegetable Silica Formula (2-3 capsules, two to three times daily).

Synergistic Vitamins and Minerals Beta-CEZB$_6$ (2 capsules, twice daily), Vitamin A (20,000 IU), B complex (two, twice daily), Vitamin C (500 mg, six times daily), Vitamin D (800 IU, twice daily), Calcium (1000 mg daily), Magnesium (500 mg, daily), Multiminerals (two, twice daily), trace minerals (two tablets, twice daily).

Gallstones

see Gravel and Stones, and Liver and Gallbladder

Giardia

see Parasites

Gout

See Arthritis.

Gravel And Stones

Gravel and stones are found most often in the gallbladder and in the kidney (renal calculi). Those formed in the gallbladder are chiefly cholesterol, indicating a toxic mucus condition that causes precipitation and hardening of this normally soluble lipid (fatty substance). In both situations the organ and its passages become blocked and the mucous membranes can become torn by the jagged edges of the stones. Infection and considerable pain are the usual results.

Recommended Action

Hydrangea root, juniper tincture and gravel root are the best solvents for kidney stones. Burdock seed and large amounts of fresh carrot juice are also good. Abstaining from solid food and drinking large quantities of juices and especially parsley root tea (by the quart) will speed results. (Do not use this treatment if pregnant). In the case of gallstones, fast for two to three days. Take a large glass of prune juice each morning to keep the bowels free and moving. During the day drink plenty of apple juice and reverse osmosis or distilled water. In the evening prepare one cup of olive oil and one cup of fresh squeezed lemon juice. Drink six tablespoons of this, thoroughly mixed, every 15 minutes until it is finished, (refer to Liver Flush in Appendix). The stones will then be passed in the stool. It is best to precede this flushing drink with one month of the Liver Formula (two capsules, three times daily). This procedure should be followed with another month of Liver Formula. **Do not** do a Liver Flush if the liver is in a very acute state.

Single Herbs Hydrangea root, Gravel root, Uva Ursi, Parsley root (kidney stone solvents).

Combinations Kidney Formula, Liver Formula.

Synergistic Vitamins and Minerals Vitamin A (10,000 IU), Choline (500 mg, essential for proper fat metabolism), Inositol (500 mg, involved in cholesterol metabolism), Biotin (25 mcg, involved in fat assimilation), B complex (including B_{12}), Vitamin C, Vitamin E (600 IU), Vitamin D (5,000 IU a week), Lecithin (2,400 mg, twice daily).

Halitosis

Halitosis, commonly known as bad breath, is caused by many factors, usually unrelated to the mouth. Although periodontal disease and dental caries can produce odor-causing bacteria, regular cleansing of the teeth, gums and tongue can usually overcome this problem. More commonly, halitosis indicates a serious underlying problem involving chemical and metabolic changes within the body. The "acetone breath" of diabetic acidosis, the premenstrual halitosis found in many women and the chronic bad breath afflicting millions with gastrointestinal problems and chronic constipation, are all examples of this type of problem. Masking the odor of bad breath with mouthwash is the equivalent of using an air freshener to solve the problem of a backed-up sewer.

Recommended Action

It is most important to avoid constipation, keeping the bowels regular and rebuilding them with the proper herbs. Exercise and a low mucus diet are also helpful. Concentrated alfalfa or liquid chlorophyll or chlorella taken daily will sweeten the stomach and intestinal tract. Drinking plenty of distilled water daily is often the only solution necessary for some people. Short-term symptomatic relief can be obtained through the use of cloves, parsley and watercress rather than a commercial mouthwash. After a meal heavy in a food such as garlic, one can simply suck on cloves to have sweet-smelling breath. Also see Candida Program because Candida can cause this problem.

Single Herbs Cloves, Parsley, Watercress (breath fresheners); Alfalfa, Chlorella.

Combinations Lower Bowel Tonic (to stimulate and rebuild the colon), Stomach Formula.

Synergistic Vitamins and Mineral Vitamin B_6 (50 mg), Vitamin C (500 mg, twice daily), Zinc (15-30 mg daily), Digestive Enzymes.

Suggested Program

Breakfast Digestive Enzymes (1-3 capsules), Chlorella (1,500 mg), Lower Bowel Tonic (1-3 capsules), Stomach Formula (1-2 capsules).

Supper same as breakfast

Hayfever

See Allergies.

Headaches

See also Migraines.

Headaches are most frequently caused by emotional stress or nervous tension but are also symptoms of allergies, poor circulation, digestive disturbance, poor ventilation or improper respiration, anemia, hypoglycemia, general infection or head injury. Chronic constipation is one of the most common causes of recurring headaches. Migraine headaches (see section on Migraines), which are usually accompanied by nausea, vomiting and visual disturbance, result from unusual constriction of the arteries to the brain, leading to a kind of cellular starvation (ischemia). The dilation of the blood vessels causes the typical throbbing pain.

Recommended Action

Realize that headaches only indicate a deeper problem and while anodyne and sedative herbs can help to relax tense nerves and relieve pain, they do not solve the problem. Use the Lower Bowel Tonic to relieve the bowels if constipation is present (enemas should be reserved for emergencies). If the stomach is the source of the problem, use an emetic to empty it. The most effective solution to any headache is rest ... and hops, peppermint and chamomile teas will usually induce a restful sleep.

Single Herbs Feverfew, Lobelia Extract (relaxant, sedative in small amounts, emetic in large amounts); Ginger (for menstrual problems); Hops (sedative, nervine to produce sleep).

Combinations Feverfew Plus Formula, Nerve Formula, Lower Bowel Tonic (constipation), Muscle Relaxing Formula (general tension).

Synergistic Vitamins and Minerals B complex, Vitamin C, Calcium, Magnesium, Magnesium Phosphate (6X) tissue salt.

Suggested Program

Feverfew Plus Formula (1-2 capsules, once or twice per day)
Muscle Relaxing Formula (2-3 capsules, three times daily)
Consider 12-day D-Tox Diet.

Heart

Improper diet and a lack of exercise are common causes of heart problems. The heart becomes overburdened as a result of poor circulation, a bloodstream loaded with impurities and a sluggish system. Our sedentary lifestyles saddle the heart muscle with unnecessary adipose (fatty) tissue, and the extra layers of fat on the body require many more miles of capillaries to supply blood and nutrients to the superfluous cells. The chances of heart failure or of acute heart attack are increased by arteriosclerosis and high blood pressure.

Recommended Action

A teaspoon of cayenne pepper in a glass of warm water is an effective first aid remedy for an acute heart attack. If the victim is still conscious, and able to drink it, this will regulate the heartbeat. If cayenne is unavailable, black pepper may be substituted but requires three times as much to achieve the same results. Regular and vigorous exercise is the primary preventative heart care measure. Remember to start off slowly! It is also important to avoid salt, sugar, alcohol, coffee, meat and all refined carbohydrates in the diet. Supplements such as

Herbal programs have good success with heart problems

The heart is a very strong organ and can regenerate rather quickly. By following the accompanying suggested program we have watched hundreds of people regain good solid heart health, within a year.

Vitamin E and lecithin are very beneficial to the heart, and potassium is critical to the proper function of all muscles, including the heart. Daily doses of elderberry extract will supply the necessary potassium. Cayenne and hawthorn berry are the two most important foods for the heart. A malfunctioning thyroid gland is often linked with heart and circulatory problems. In a sense this is the master regulator of all the body's systems and so should be fed and strengthened with appropriate herbs. Reishi is a herb that can both strengthen the heart and calm it down. It is excellent for heart arrhythmia.

Single Herbs Cayenne, Cayenne Extract, Reishi, Garlic, Hawthorn Berry, Elderberry Extract.

Combinations Hawthorn Plus Formula, Reishi Plus Formula, Cayenne Plus Formula.

Synergistic Vitamins and Minerals Vitamin B_3, Vitamin B_6, B complex, Vitamin B_{15}, Vitamin C, Vitamin E, Selenium, Calcium/ Magnesium, Potassium, Zinc, Copper, Chromium.

Suggested Program

One of the most important causes of circulatory problems is free radical degeneration of the arterial walls. This degeneration puts a large strain on the heart and all of the following foods have the potential to enhance free radicals and should therefore be avoided:

preservatives, food dyes, partly saturated vegetable oils (especially margarine), rancid oils, chlorinated water, cola drinks, high sugar beverages, coffee, tea (most herb teas are alright), table salt (including sea salt), alcohol, protein-carbohydrate combinations, smoked meat, cooking with vegetable oils.

The following guidelines should also be adhered to:

1. Roughage should always be present.
2. Meals should be small and fairly frequent. Avoid large meals.
3. Food should be chewed extremely well.

Breakfast a grain with 1 tablespoon of flax seed or other polyunsaturated oil and "lite" soya sauce. 1 Multiminerals, 1 Multivitamins and minerals, 1 B complex, Ester C (500 mg), Selenium (100-200 mcg), 1 Calcium/Magnesium tablet, Hawthorn Plus Formula (2-3 capsules), Cayenne Plus Formula (1-2 capsules), Reishi Plus Formula (3 capsules).

Lunch a salad or soup. Vitamin E (start with 100 IU and build up to 400 IU), Vitamin C (500 mg).

Supper a salad with grains, lightly cooked vegetables and/or some fish or lean poultry. Supplements Same as at breakfast.

Before retiring Vitamin E (gradually build up to 400 IU).

Hemorrhoids

Often known as "piles", this condition involves varicose (enlarged) veins of the anal or rectal area. Weak blood vessels in that area, constipation, straining during elimination, a life-style that involves too much sitting and a calcium deficiency are indicated in this situation. They are usually accompanied by itching, and if the condition is uncared for, prolapsus of the anal wall, rupture of small veins and secondary infection may result.

Good-bye Hemorrhoids

The best herbal for hemorrhoids is Fargelin (a Chinese formula) which has the ability to work as an astringent on varicose veins. To avoid hemorrhoids the bowels must be kept active. Fel Ursi is a good pile ointment. Collisonia root taken orally and plantain ointment also work well.

Recommended Action

It is very important to avoid constipation. Change to a diet low in mucus and use the Lower Bowel Tonic. Regular exercise and drinking plenty of steam distilled or reverse osmosis water daily will help. Apply Vitamin E or wheat germ oil to the area; they may be taken orally as well. Even better results will be found using plantain or collinsonia ointment and suppositories. A White oak bark and collinsonia root enema has been shown to be useful in this condition.

Single Herbs Collinsonia Root, Garlic, Mullein, Plantain, White Oak Bark.

Combinations Lower Bowel Tonic, Psyllax, Fargelin, Fel Ursi Ointment.

Synergistic Vitamins and Minerals Vitamin C (1,000 mg, three times daily), Bioflavonoids (1,000 mg,twice daily)

Hepatitis

see Liver and Gallbladder

Herpes

These single to multiple, small fluid-filled blisters cause local burning or stinging pain. They can be found about the mouth (herpes gingivostomatitis), lips (herpes labialis), genitals (herpes genitalis) and eyes (herpes keratoconjuctivitis). After a person is initially infected, the virus will remain in a dormant state in the nervous system until another outbreak. Herpes will sometimes reoccur after minor infections, trauma, stress (emotional, dietary or environmental) and sun exposure. The incubation period is two to twelve days (averaging six to ten), with a typical infection lasting one to two weeks. It is hard to say how many people are affected with dormant herpes (estimates range from 20-100%), There are more than 70 viruses in the herpes family. The chance of getting herpes from intimate contact with a person with active herpes is estimated to be roughly 70%. It is interesting to note that some people never get herpes when in contact with partners with herpes. This suggests that the state of the immune system plays an important role in the contagion for herpes.

Recommended Action

The most important factor in dealing with herpes is that of immunity. It appears if a person's immune system is strong enough when coming into contact with herpes, they will not contract it. If a person already has herpes laying dormant in the nervous system, good immunity and general health (physically and psychologically) will lower the incidence of recurrence. Once a person has herpes, it appears to be unlikely that they will ever rid the body of the virus. It is quite possible to keep the herpes in a dormant state for many years though.

Since lack of lysine is noted in people during herpes outbreaks, foods high in arginine (a lysine antagonist) should be avoided during outbreaks or even high stress. Foods high in arginine include almonds, barley, cashews, grains, chicken, chocolate, corn, dairy products, meat, nuts and seeds, oats and peanuts. Citrus fruit has been alleged to extend the length of a herpes outbreak.

Single Herbs Licorice, Echinacea, Myrrh, Red Clover, Goldenseal, St. John's Wort, Essential Fatty Acids.

Combinations Glycyrrhizic Acid (from licorice)/Menthol mixture, Chinese White Flower Embrocation (Pak Fah Yeow), yellow (classic) Listerine® soaked onto the area.

Synergistic Vitamins and Minerals Beta-CEZB$_6$ (2-3 tablets, two-three times daily), Beta-carotene (100,000 IU daily), B complex (1 tablet, twice daily), Vitamin C (1,000 mg, twice daily), Bioflavonoids (1,000 mg daily), Vitamin E (400 IU daily), Zinc (15-60 mg daily), Lysine (2 gm daily).

Social Stigma and Herpes

There is a strong social stigma surrounding genital herpes. Sufferers feel almost like social outcasts. With the high number of people with herpes, reconsideration of this might be in order. Herpes is not contagious unless in an active stage. It can often be active in a hidden area of the body though. Some feel that herpes is a good monitor of how well a person's body is handling the stress they are under.

Suggested Program

Breakfast Beta-CEZB$_6$ (2-3 tablets), Goldenseal Plus Formula (2 capsules), Lysine (1,000 mg). Apply Listerine® or Glycyrrhizic acid ointment or Inflammation Ointment on area.
Supper Repeat supplement from breakfast

High Blood Pressure

Arteriosclerosis, obesity, stress, excessive salt intake, nervous tension, kidney malfunction and many other factors make it necessary for the heart to work harder in order to pump blood and nutrients to the various body parts. In an attempt to defend itself and correct the situation, the body responds with high blood pressure, otherwise known as hypertension. As this is a symptomatic condition, an attempt to identify and resolve the cause is necessary before attempting to eliminate the symptom.

Recommended Action

Herbs like cayenne, garlic, sassafras and the herbal formula "Reishi Plus Formula" dissolve and remove deposits of precipitated impurities. Avoid mucus forming foods which clog up the bloodstream. It is also wise to avoid overeating, tension and stress, and to eliminate any excess weight. Juice fasts are beneficial if properly conducted. Ensure that the heart and circulatory system are properly nourished. For more information see Heart and Arteriosclerosis.

High Blood Pressure

Over the years there have been many cases of people coming in with high blood pressure. Mr. T. is a good example. He had a blood pressure of 210/130. He took three Reishi plus, one capsule of cayenne pepper during meals, one garlic/parsley capsule twice daily, Vitamin C (2000 mg with 1000 mg of Bioflavonoids), Vitamin E (200 IU). His diet excluded all dairy and flour products, salt, fried foods and preservatives. We suggested that he eat lots of whole grains, fish and raw vegetables. In three months his blood pressure was down to 160/100, and in nine months it was 135/90, at which time we slowly lowered his therapy.

Single Herbs Reishi, Cayenne or Cayenne Extract, Garlic, Ginger, Hawthorn Berry Syrup or Tincture, Elderberry Extract.

Combinations Reishi Plus Formula, Cayenne Plus Formula.

Synergistic Vitamins and Minerals Vitamin C (500 mg, two to six times daily); Bioflavonoids (250 mg, two to six times daily); Vitamin E (start with 100 IU gradually increasing to 400 - 800 IU daily); Lecithin (1200 mg, two times daily); Calcium (1500 mg); Magnesium (200-500 mg); Multivitamins and minerals.

Suggested Program

Breakfast Reishi Plus Formula (3 capsules), Cayenne Plus Formula (1 capsule), Garlic (2 capsules), Beta-CEZB$_6$ (2 tablets)

Lunch Vitamin E (200 IU)
Supper same as breakfast

Ginger root tea is good to drink with this problem.

Hiccups

Spasmodic contractions of the diaphragm cause sudden inhalation, followed by a sudden closing of the glottis which produces the "hic" sound. Irritation of the phrenic nerves controlling the diaphragm causes the condition, the irritation often being an overloaded stomach or a sudden emotional change. Singultus is the clinical term for hiccups.

Recommended Action

To relax the nerves and relieve contractions take a few drops of Lobelia Extract on the tongue or in a glass of water.

Single Herbs Lobelia Extract.

Hives

see Herpes

Follow the program listed for herpes. A bath in ginger root tea, followed with a sponge bath in chamomile tea, can be very therapeutic. The use of Glycyrrhizic Acid/Menthol Ointment has been very useful in this area. Inflammation Ointment is very soothing, taking away most of the stinging.

Hormone Imbalance

If one or more of the endocrine glands (pineal, pituitary, thyroid, parathyroid, pancreas, adrenal or reproductive) becomes over- or underactive, hormone imbalances result. Hormones are the chemical regulators of the body's systems and are produced by the aforementioned glands. Major body functions become upset when any one of the above glands produces too much or too little of a particular hormone in relation to others. Often the results can be disastrous.

Hormones and Hair Loss

Hormone imbalances are often responsible for hair loss in both men and women. Women often start to lose hair between eight and fourteen months after delivering a child. This can usually be traced to a hormone imbalance. The loss of hair in men can have many causes, but one fairly common one is an excess of male hormones. In both men and women the reversal of hair loss, if begun at an early stage, can often be achieved by taking herbal supplements. A good program would be Female Formula (two, three times daily); two Multiminerals, twice daily; Vitamin E (400 IU daily); plenty of grains, fruits and fresh vegetables.

Recommended Action

Avoid all refined carbohydrates as these have a tendency to throw the glandular machinery off balance. For herbal hormone supplements use those in the following paragraphs.

Single Herbs Chlorella, Alfalfa (pituitary); Licorice root, Siberian Ginseng (adrenals); Cedar Berries (pancreas); Dulse, Kelp (thyroid); Mullein (all glands); Ginseng, Sarsaparilla (male); Dong Quai, Blessed Thistle, Black Cohosh (female).

Combinations Female Formula (for males and females, especially during puberty, pregnancy, menopause, male "change of life", and after stopping birth control pills).

Synergistic Vitamins and Minerals Vitamin A, B complex, Vitamin B_6 (75 mg daily), Zinc, Calcium, Magnesium.

Hypoglycemia

Hypoglycemia is defined as a low level of glucose (blood sugar) in the bloodstream. It can be caused by an overproduction of insulin or by a malfunction of the adrenal glands. The former results in too rapid a utilization of glucose by the body's cells, while the latter results in overstressed adrenal glands.

A person with low blood sugar will usually show one or more of the following symptoms: a strong craving for sweets or starches; emotional ups and downs; tiredness most of the time, especially in the late afternoon or after eating; stress; easy blow-ups; tiredness upon waking, even with a full night's sleep; difficulty in getting to sleep even when tired; frequent headaches. Hypoglycemia is extremely common in North America because of both our diets and our stress levels. Some authorities estimate it to affect as much as 40% of the population!

Low Blood Sugar

If the accompanying suggested program is followed along with the complex carbohydrate diet in the Appendix and stress levels are lowered, the average hypoglycemic will be able to be symptom-free with just a very few maintenance supplements in 12-18 months. If reflexology is added to the program with counselling feedback every two to three weeks, the same results can usually be obtained in six to nine months.

Recommended Action

The most important things for low blood sugar (LBS) is to avoid sweets, alleviate the stress, and lessen the overactivity of the pancreas. One of the most common therapies on the market is a high protein diet. I am strongly against this in most cases. In fact, I feel this type of therapy can often lead to diabetes by overstimulating the system. The therapy that I strongly support is a high proportion of complex carbohydrates. In the Appendix you will find the Complex Carbohydrate Diet that we suggest for people with LBS problems. It is quite important for these people to eat regularly, so we suggest three meals a day with three snacks. Surprisingly, in doing so, a person will often lose rather than gain weight.

Single Herbs Devil's Club, Cedar Berries (pancreas); Licorice Root, Uva Ursi leaves (adrenals).

Combinations Glucose Formula, Four Ginsengs.

Synergistic Vitamins and Minerals B complex, Vitamin C, Vitamin E, Multivitamins and minerals, Nucleic acid, Chromium.

Suggested Program

Follow the Complex Carbohydrate Diet (see Appendix).

Breakfast B complex (1 tablet), Glucose Formula (2 capsules), Ener-Jazz (1 tsp.), Reishi Plus Formula (2 capsules), Multivitamins and minerals (1 tablet), Chromium (1 tablet, if indicated), Four Ginsengs (1 capsule).

Morning Snack Vitamin C (500 mg)

Lunch Vitamin E (400 IU), Vitamin C (500 mg), Glucose Formula (2 capsules), Ener-Jazz (1/2 tsp.)

Afternoon Snack Vitamin C (500 mg)

Supper Same as breakfast

Evening snack Vitamin C (500 mg)

Impotence And Frigidity

The term impotence is usually used in reference to males and means either the lack of desire or the inability to perform the sex act satisfactorily, in spite of desire. The term frigidity is usually used in reference to females to indicate the same condition, but may also be used to describe a female totally lacking in interest. The problem for either sex is often psychological in nature and, ironically, is found with increasing frequency in our "liberated" society. It is also possible, however, for it to be due to nutritional and metabolic imbalances or to physical injury. Candida yeast infection can be a common cause.

Recommended Action

If physical injury is not the problem, change to a diet as follows: avoid all refined carbohydrates and eat mainly fresh fruits and vegetables, whole grains, nuts and seeds. Take Vitamin E, wheat germ oil, ginseng or Siberian ginseng as a supplement, and drink plenty of distilled or reverse osmosis water.

Male Impotence

The occurrence of male impotence is much higher than most people think. Here is an example: A fairly successful businessman, in his mid-forties, under too much stress, complains that his sex life isn't what it used to be. In fact, his wife is starting to complain about it. He started taking Four Ginsengs, Vitamin E (400 IU, twice daily), Kidney/Bladder Formula (two capsules, twice daily). In his diet he eliminated all preservatives, food dyes, simple carbohydrates and fried foods. Within one month his wife stopped complaining. In two months, they were thanking me.

Single herbs Ginseng (stimulates all endocrine glands), Bee Pollen (builds up both male and female organs), Orchid (strengthens sexual desires, especially in males), Buchu (strengthens prostate), Kava Kava (for females).

Combinations Female Formula (hormone balancer for both males and females); Ener-Jazz (stimulates sexual activity); Kidney Formula (strengthen male organs); Men's Formula, Four Ginsengs (males and females), Muscle Relaxing Formula (females).

Synergistic Vitamins and Minerals Vitamin A (10,000 IU, twice daily), B complex, Vitamin B_6 (50-75 mg), PABA (100 mg), Vitamin C (500 mg, three times daily), Vitamin E (200-600 IU), Zinc (25-75 mg).

Suggested Program

Breakfast Female Formula (2 capsules), Four Ginsengs (3 capsules), Multivitamins and minerals (1 tablet), Beta-CEZB_6 (1 tablet), Men's Formula (2 capsules); Muscle Relaxing Formula (2-3 capsules, for females).
Snack Ener-Jazz (1 tsp.), Ester C (500 mg).
Lunch Multivitamins and minerals (1 tablet)
Snack same as morning
Supper same as breakfast

Infection

Bacteria, viruses or fungi are usually present in the environment and in the body itself. By themselves these microorganisms pose no serious threat, but when they begin to multiply in accumulated toxic wastes or deteriorating tissue, infection is said to exist. The blood rushes in to supply white blood cells and other elements in an attempt to contain the infection and repair damaged tissue. This results in the characteristic redness and swelling of inflammation.

Recommended Action

Disease germs serve a useful role in cleaning up the internal environment and recycling wastes, but it is most important that they be kept under control. Antiseptic and antibiotic herbs, as well as anthelmintics and febrifuges, are used for this purpose. Refer to specific section for infections in those areas.

Single Herbs Goldenseal, Echinacea, Myrrh (antiseptic); Garlic (antibiotic); Black Walnut (anthelmintic); Thyme, Fenugreek (febrifuges).

Combinations Cleansing Formula, Goldenseal Plus Formula, Echinacea Plus Formula.

Synergistic Vitamins and Minerals Beta-CEZB$_6$, Vitamin A (20,000 IU, twice daily), Vitamin C (500 mg, six times daily).

Infertility

This is the inability to conceive children and may be due to problems with either partner. In females, the common causes range from malnutrition, structural problems in the reproductive organs, scarred Fallopian tubes (from pelvic inflammatory disease), hormone imbalances, inability to ovulate, or advanced age. Emotional issues can also be a contributing factor. In males, the cause can be related to low sperm count, motility and penetration; abnormally-shaped sperm; insufficient seminal fluid; undescended testicles; injured testicles; childhood disease (such as mumps); infection, and prostate disorders.

Nutritional deficiencies, radiation (too many X-rays), and heavy metal toxicity can also be contributing factors in both ovum and sperm dysfunction.

Too much of a good thing can cause Infertility

We all know that a high fat diet without exercise is bad for health. Some people take this too far and have absolutely no fat in their diet, doing 30-60 minutes of aerobic exercise daily. This can cause a woman to have irregular cycles and not produce healthy eggs to fertilize. Some types of fat are essential in our diet.

Recommended Action

If a period of more than twelve months has gone by without pregnancy, physical examinations are appropriate (to determine sperm count, pelvic inflammation, etc.). It is possible other glandular systems (especially the thyroid) might be involved. It is often hard for females who exercise excessively to get pregnant.

It is of course important to eat as whole a diet as possible, both preceding and during pregnancy. The elimination of processed food, alcohol, cigarette and excessive caffeine should be implemented. It is often best to detoxify the body before trying to get pregnant (see D-Tox Diet in Appendix). A hair analysis will determine if there is any heavy mineral toxicity. It is important to make sure the liver and the bowels are not sluggish.

Single Herbs Females: Dong Quai, False Unicorn (*Helonias*), Vitex, Siberian Ginseng, Royal Jelly, Ground Ivy. Males: Ginseng, Siberian Ginseng.

Combinations

Females: Female Formula, Essential Fatty Acids (200-400 mg, gamma-linolenic acid daily), Chinese Phoenix Formula (Wuchi PaiFeng Wan, Women's Tea), Fertility tea.

Males: Four Ginsengs, Men's Formula, Ashwaghandha, Fertility tea.

Synergistic Vitamins and Minerals

Female: BetaCEZB$_6$ (2 tablets, twice daily), Beta-carotene (20,000 IU, twice daily), B complex (1 tablet, twice daily), Vitamin B$_6$ (20-500 mg daily), Vitamin C (at least 3,000 mg daily), Vitamin E (400 IU daily), Zinc (15-60 mg daily), Magnesium (at least 400 mg daily).

Males: The above supplements also work well for males. Men often don't need as much Vitamin B$_6$, but more zinc. Sometimes the addition of the amino acid arginine (up to 1,000 mg, if no herpes present) is useful.

Insomnia

The inability to fall asleep or to stay asleep long enough to obtain sufficient rest is called insomnia, and is often caused by emotional stress, nervous tension, physical aches and pains, meals eaten late at night, mental activity late at night, and stimulants such as are found in coffee, tea, and cola drinks. Hypoglycemia, Candida or adrenal exhaustion will often manifest as insomnia.

Daytime activities can cause insomnia

Often peoples' lives get them all speeded up during the day. By overstimulating the mind all day long, it is often hard to slow it down at night. Taking calming herbs during the day can relax the mind so it can have a deeper sleep. A calm mind during the day can also allow a person to be more productive during daylight hours. The best herb for this has been Reishi (3 capsules, two-three times daily).

Recommended Action

Avoid all drugs and sleeping pills (consult a practitioner before coming off sleeping pills), as they not only create an unnatural dependence but also further disturb the dream pattern and can cause neurosis. Avoid late meals and mental activity and make an effort not to worry about problems as this will only contribute to insomnia. Try taking a leisurely walk (especially barefoot, to discharge the static electricity built up in the body during the day), a warm bath or a meditation before bed. These measures can help to remove the insomnia and establish new patterns of restful sleep. Refer also to the sections on hypoglycemia or Candida for treatment when this apparently is the prime cause.

Single Herbs Reishi, Hops, Lady's Slipper root, Valerian root, Passionflower, Chamomile, Skullcap.

Combinations Valerian Plus Formula, Reishi Plus Formula, Nerve Formula, Sleeping Formula.

Synergistic Vitamins and Minerals B complex, Multivitamins and minerals, Multiminerals, Trace minerals, Calcium, Magnesium, Melatonin (1-6 mg).

Suggested Program

Breakfast Reishi Plus Formula (3 capsules), Nerve Formula (2 capsules).
Lunch same as breakfast
Supper same as breakfast
30 min before bed Valerian Plus Formula (2-3 capsules), Melatonin (3-6 mg).

Irritable Bowel Syndrome

(see also Colitis, Crohn's Disease, Constipation and Diarrhea)

Kidney And Bladder

Infection is usually the cause of kidney and bladder problems. Waste products from body processes are filtered out of the blood by the kidneys, which also regulate the fluid and electrolyte balance in the body. The wastes and excess electrolytes which are excreted, along with water, in the form of urine, are retained in the bladder until voiding. Cystitis refers to an inflammation of the bladder, whether it involves actual infection or not. Frequent, urgent and painful urination (sometimes with blood or pus) and pain in the lower abdomen and back area are symptoms of cystitis. Nephritis refers to an inflammation of the nephrons in the kidney, leading to the deterioration of that organ and sometimes death. It is nearly always a result of bacterial infection. Bright's disease refers to several extreme forms of glomerulonephritis which involves degeneration of the kidney's minute filter cells. The acute form of this disease is generally preceded by a streptococcus infection somewhere in the body and there may be no overt symptoms. However, in most cases of kidney disease, chills, fever, headache and blood or albumen (blood plasma protein) in the urine accompany the pain and tenderness in the kidney area. Kidney problems may also be indicated by edema and high blood pressure. See "Gravel and Stones" for a discussion of kidney stones.

Recommended Action

Initially, one should do a juice fast (like the Lemon Aid Cleanse), followed by a diet low in mucus and containing at least 1/2 gallon of steam distilled or reverse osmosis water daily. Watermelon (especially its seeds) is beneficial. Potent diuretics tone and stimulate the entire urinary tract, most notably the kidneys. Remember, don't push the kidneys too hard! If there is bleeding in the urinary tract, use marshmallow, which is a specific homeostatic in this case. If it is severe, simmer one ounce marshmallow root in one pint of milk and drink a half-cup every half hour until the bleeding stops, continue taking a half-cup every hour for the rest of the day. To ensure that the organ is healing, take this remedy three times a day for the next three days. If kidney problems are complicated by, or are a result of prostate or menstrual difficulties, those problems should also be dealt with specifically at the same time. Consult a practitioner if complications occur.

Single Herbs Parsley, Juniper Berries, Dandelion Root, Uva Ursi, Gravel Root (diuretic and kidney function), Cat's Claw.

Combinations Kidney/Bladder Formula, Cranberry Concentrate Plus Formula, Goldenseal Plus Formula.

Synergistic Vitamins and Minerals Bcta-CEZB_6 (2 tablets, twice daily), Beta-carotene (80,000 IU daily for three months, then lowered to 20,000 IU), Vitamin B_6 (50 mg), Vitamin B_2 (25 mg), Choline (500-1000 mg), Vitamin C (500 mg, three to six times daily), Vitamin E (200-1000 IU daily), Potassium (one to five grams of Potassium Chloride), Lecithin (1200 mg, twice daily).

Suggested Program

Breakfast Kidney/Bladder Formula (2 capsules), Beta-CEZB$_6$ (2 tablets).
Lunch Kidney/Bladder Formula (2 capsules)
Supper same as breakfast
Add Cranberry Concentrate Plus Formula if there is bladder infection.

Lactation

Lactation is the production of milk by the female breasts, in most cases brought on by the sucking of the infant. There may be times, however, when it is necessary to take advantage of the extra assistance afforded by the galactagogue herbs which promote and enrich the flow of milk. Drinking a lot of distilled water will also help.

Single Herbs Blessed Thistle, Marshmallow Root.

Combinations Female Formula (two or three times daily for six weeks), TanKwe Gin (1 tbsp., 2 times daily for two bottles).

Synergistic Vitamins and Minerals Vitamin A (20,000 IU), Vitamin D (800 IU), Multivitamins and minerals (one tablet, twice daily), Calcium (250 mg, twice daily), Magnesium (125 mg, twice daily), trace minerals.

Blessed Thistle ... Might Be Too Much!

When taking Blessed Thistle to bring in milk or just to build up supplies, start off slowly. I had one student who was going to wetnurse for a friend over a weekend. To ensure that she would have enough for both her own child and her friend's she took four capsules of Blessed Thistle and two cups of Blessed Thistle tea. Within a day she felt she was going to burst. Both babies just couldn't keep up with her production of milk.

I have also had three students who all tell the same story about how they adopted children, took Blessed Thistle and marshmallow tea and started producing milk within three days. All experienced a fair bit of pain in their breasts but all felt it was worth it.

Laryngitis

Inflammation of the larynx or voice box is known as laryngitis. It can be due to the irritation of air pollutants, emotional stress or allergic reaction but is more often the result of bacterial or viral infection or, sometimes, from just plain overwork.

Recommended Action

Mucus discharge by the inflamed membranes causes the hoarseness of laryngitis because it interferes with the normal vibration of the vocal cords. Take lemon juice and honey (equal parts either alone or mixed with water). This will relieve hoarseness while demulcent and expectorant herbs will soothe the area. The best demulcent for soothing the throat is Slippery Elm and Zinc Lozenges which can be obtained in most health food stores.

Single Herbs Licorice Root, Slippery Elm (for hoarseness); Ginger (for soreness); Goldenseal, Echinacea, Garlic (for infection).

Combinations Fomentation of 3 parts Mullein and 1 part Lobelia (to the neck and throat, for soreness), Goldenseal Plus Formula.

Synergistic Vitamins and Minerals Beta-CEZB$_6$ (3 tablets, three times daily), Beta-carotene (30,000 IU, twice daily), B complex (two, twice daily), Vitamin C (500 mg, six times daily), Zinc (15-75 mg daily).

Liver And Gallbladder

Liver and gallbladder function is essential not only to proper digestion and elimination, but also to overall body metabolism. The liver is, among other things, the body's "Master Filter", cleansing the blood of impurities and poisons, neutralizing them and transforming them into bile, an excretory fluid that has a key role as a natural laxative, intestinal alkalizer, and fat emulsifier and digestant. Bile is stored in the gallbladder until it is needed. Then it is squirted through the bile duct into the upper part of the small intestine. If the bile becomes obstructed, pain and digestive disturbances result, along with a condition called jaundice. Gallstones are often responsible for this condition, which is characterized by yellow and itching skin, and yellow in the whites of the eyes, as bile salts escape into the blood and are excreted through the skin. Infection of the liver, known as hepatitis, also produces the symptoms of jaundice. Cirrhosis of the liver involves the destruction of the liver cells and their replacement by scar tissue, which gradually renders the organ unable to function and unless reversed in time, results in death. It is caused by malnutrition, fatty accumulations in the liver, and the toxic effect of excessive alcohol consumption on the liver cells. Age spots, also known as liver spots, commonly appear on exposed areas of the skin as people grow older and their livers begin to function less effectively. They seem to disappear, however, as the liver is restored to full function and the blood is cleansed. Cancers and tumors seem to be connected with an inability of the liver to carry out its normal function of neutralizing poisons and detoxifying the system.

Recommended Action

A juice fast followed by the Inner Cleanse Diet (see Appendix) is a first step to clean out and rebuild a malfunctioning liver. All processed and canned foods, as well as all chemical additives, synthetic vitamins, etc. should be strictly avoided. Hepatic and cholagogue herbs, along with a few specific liver alteratives, will stimulate and rebuild the organ. Castor oil fomentations and clay packs are excellent aids, and advantage should be taken of them. Red beets and beet juice or powder are especially beneficial, as is lemon juice, papaya juice and grape juice.

Gallbladder Stones

After doing the accompanying Liver Flush you will often see hundreds of little green balls in the toilet. Some think that these are the gallstones, but they are not. They are cholesterol balls which do represent a thorough cleansing of the gallbladder and liver. Sometimes smaller hard black or reddish colored stones accompany these green balls. These were probably what was giving you the pain.

Single Herbs Black Radish (builder, cleanser, regulator); Milk Thistle, Barberry (liver tonic); Beet powder, Dandelion, Goldenseal root, Gravel Root, Parsley (hepatics and cholagogues).

Combinations Liver Formula (rebuilds liver); Kidney/Bladder Formula (helps to strengthen liver and spleen); Lower Bowel Tonic (cleansing and detoxifying); Cleansing Formula (detoxifies).

Synergistic Vitamins and Minerals Vitamin A (20,000 to 40,000 IU), B complex (high potency), Vitamin B_6 (50 mg), Vitamin B_{12} (50 mcg), Niacin (100 mg), Vitamin C (2,000 to 4,000 mg), Vitamin E (400 IU), Lecithin (9,600 mg).

Suggested Program

If the liver is not in an acute state, use Liver Flush after the three day Cleansing Diet (see Appendix).

Breakfast Liver Formula (2 capsules), Beta-CEZB_6 (2 tablets), Reishi Plus Formula (2 capsules).
Snack Vitamin C (500 mg), Lecithin (1200 mg).
Lunch Vitamin C (500 mg), Vitamin E (400 IU).
Snack Vitamin C (500 mg), Lecithin (2,400 mg).
Supper Same as Breakfast

Low Blood Pressure

Low blood pressure or hypotension, can be a sign of a long and healthy life. On the other hand, if it is accompanied by fainting, dizziness, anemia, bleeding or excessive fatigue, it may be a symptom of tuberculosis, cancer, low blood sugar, rheumatism, or adrenal, thyroid, or pituitary insufficiency.

Recommended Action

If hypotension is symptomatic of another disorder, that condition will need to be resolved first, or at least simultaneously. The best tonic for low blood pressure is regular exercise and lots of deep breathing. Herbal aids include mainly blood cleansers and builders.

Single Herbs Beet Powder, Dandelion, Garlic, Ginseng, Sassafras, Cayenne.

Combinations Four Ginsengs, Ener-Jazz, Cayenne Plus Formula.

Lungs

The lungs provide oxygen to the bloodstream and expel the waste carbon dioxide. Body temperature is also partly maintained by the process of respiration. Asthma and bronchitis (dealt with in detail elsewhere) are conditions which interfere with this process. Bronchitis, which is characterized by difficult breathing along with coughing, wheezing and the spitting up of mucus, is an inflammation of the bronchial tubes (air passages of the lungs). It can be acute (almost always a complication of an upper respiratory infection) or chronic (usually a result of smoking, air pollution, or a symptom of a more severe problem such as emphysema). Emphysema involves structural damage to the alveoli (tiny exchange mechanisms which are designed to get oxygen into the blood). A more or less constant sensation of suffocation comes from inhalation, followed by the inability to exhale. In pneumonia, the tiny air sacs (alveoli) become filled with fluid, usually as a result of bacterial or viral infection. The body responds with inflammation and the generation of fluids which interfere with oxygen intake. Pleurisy, usually a complication of other inflammatory conditions, is infection of the sac-like membrane surrounding the lungs and pleural cavity. This causes pus, other fluids and sometimes fibrous material to be exuded into the chest cavity.

Recommended Action

The bowels must be kept free and moving in order to detoxify the system, and a liquid diet should be adhered to. The appropriate herbs should be used to keep the bacterial and viral infections under control. Congestion of the chest and lungs can be effectively relieved by the use of poultices (such as mustard packs), fomentations, clay packs, etc., while demulcent and expectorant herbs soothe the inflamed membranes and aid in expelling the mucous secretions.

Single Herbs Slippery Elm, Licorice Root, Marshmallow Root, Mullein, Comfrey (demulcent and expectorant), Goldenseal, Garlic, Echinacea, Myrrh Gum (antiseptic), Reishi (tonic).

Combinations Lung Formula, Reishi Plus Formula, Goldenseal Plus Formula.

Synergistic Vitamins and Minerals Beta-CEZB$_6$ (2 tablets, twice daily), Beta-carotene (20,000 IU, twice daily), Vitamin C (500 mg, six times daily), Multivitamins and minerals.

Suggested Program

Lung Formula (3 capsules, 3 times daily)
Reishi Plus Formula (3 capsules, 3 times daily)
Beta-CEZB$_6$ (2 tablets, twice daily)
if infection, add Goldenseal Plus Formula (2 capsules, twice daily)

Follow a mucusless diet.

Lymphatic System

One of the body's major lines of defense against infection, this one-way system pulls fluids, plasma protein and other matter from the intercellular spaces into its capillaries, which are found virtually everywhere in the body. This lymph flows from the capillaries into progressively larger lymphatic vessels, passing periodically through small filters called lymph nodes - the familiar "glands" that get so swollen and tender when infection is present in the body. Their normal function is to neutralize and eliminate any poisons or infectious microbes that may be present. However, during acute infection they can become overworked, swollen and sore. If the lymphatic system isn't functioning up to par, it may lose the battle and the nodes themselves become the centers of infection.

A sluggish lymphatic system which no longer effectively fulfils its function is quite possibly responsible for the resulting waste retention. Down the road this might lead to an accumulation of toxins resulting in gout, arthritis, or even cancer, heart disease and other "degenerative" diseases.

Recommended Action

Deep breathing and aerobic exercise, the best tonics for a sluggish lymphatic system, will help it to pump more effectively. Vigorous massage and bouncing on a rebounder can also stimulate it. Using a fomentation of 3 parts mullein and 1 part lobelia for swollen glands and drinking a tea of the same will often help. Most kidney teas will help take the stress off the lymphatic system when drunk cool to cold. Taken hot they can be used to actively cleanse the system.

Single Herbs Mullein (specific for glands); Goldenseal, Echinacea, Myrrh Gum, Plantain (infection fighters).

Combinations Cleansing Formula, three parts Mullein with one part Lobelia, Kidney/Bladder Formula.

Synergistic Vitamins and Minerals Beta-carotene (10,000 IU, twice daily), Vitamin B_6 (75 mg), Vitamin E (200-400 IU), Multivitamins and minerals, Multitissue salts (especially Nat. Mur.).

Measles

The major characteristic of this contagious disease is a reddish skin rash which is common to both of its two forms. Rubella ("German" or "Three-day" measles), has a light pink rash that fades in three or four days and does not peel. It sometimes doesn't even appear. The symptoms, such as head cold and cough, are mild and the fever is not too high. The glands behind the ears usually swell and there may be pain in the joints for about a week.

The second, rubeola ("Common" or "Seven-day" measles), is more serious and more likely to involve complications. It is characterized by fever, cough, inflammation of the eyes and tiny red patches (with white crystal-like centers) inside the cheeks and mouth. These last are definite indications of rubeola and are called Koplik's spots. The rash, which eventually peels, appears a few days later as small red spots surrounded by darker red patches that run together forming irregular blotches. Complications can result, such as a cough that leads to laryngitis, bronchitis or pneumonia, ear or eye infections, heart problems or inflammation of the brain (encephalitis).

Recommended Action

Take nothing but juices, distilled or reverse osmosis water and herb teas for the first few days. Keep the bowels free and moving by using Lower Bowel Tonic and/or garlic or catnip enemas. Temporary relief can be achieved by the use of saffron, which will help the rash to break out and alleviate the fever. Use goldenseal or apple cider vinegar to relieve itching of the skin. Use diaphoretic and nervine teas to help maintain the elimination of toxins through the skin and to soothe a system weary from inflammation, irritation and itching.

Single Herbs Yarrow, Chamomile, Geranium, Saffron, Eyebright, Red Raspberry leaves, Goldenseal (cleansing and diaphoretic); Siberian Ginseng.

Synergistic Vitamins and Minerals During convalescence: BETA-Plus ZB6, Beta-Carotene (20,000 IU, twice daily), Vitamin C (500 mg, twice daily), Vitamin E (400 IU).

Memory

The cerebral cortex of the brain controls memory function. Arteriosclerosis in the arteries leading to the brain, along with inorganic mineral deposits in the brain cells themselves, results in ischemia (cell starvation from lack of oxygen and nutrients). This interferes with the thinking processes and produces what is usually recognized as senile behaviour.

Recommended Action

Drink large amounts of steam-distilled or reverse osmosis water to leach out the inorganic deposits. Ensure that the brain receives proper nourishment to rebuild the deteriorating cells. Maintain and promote good circulation.

Single Herbs Ginkgo, Blue Vervain, Gotu Kola, Fo-ti-teng, Blessed Thistle (specifics for the brain).

Synergistic Vitamins and Minerals B complex (two tablets, twice daily), Beta-CEZB_6 (two tablets, twice daily) Vitamin C (500 mg, three times daily), Glutamine, Tyrosine, Lecithin (1200 mg, twice daily).

Best for Memory

By far the best herb for memory is ginkgo. It increases the amount of blood oxygen in the brain. It also increases the amount of neurotransmitter (needed for memory) and the number of receptor sites for neurotransmission in the brain. This all adds up to better memory.

Suggested Program

Ginkgo (2 capsules, three times daily), Beta-CEZB_6 (2 tablets, twice daily).

Menopause

Menopause is the cessation of menses when the uterus shrinks and the ovaries quit producing stimulating hormones. Irregular menses accompanied by "hot flashes", headaches, insomnia and general irritability often precede cessation by a few months to several years. The changes in body chemistry brought on by the reduction of certain female hormones cause these symptoms. Diminished interest in sex is often associated with menopause but is not necessarily always the case. A woman's sexual activity can often be stimulated by the diminished possibility of pregnancy.

Menopause

Mrs. M. came in with a problem of "hot flashes" from her change of life. While she was sitting in front of me she started having a sweating session which completely soaked through her wool suit. She had a severe expression of symtpoms. Upon taking three Female Formula three times daily, within six weeks she was symptom-free.

Single Herbs Dong Quai (hormone regulator), Black Cohosh, Blue Cohosh, Blessed Thistle, Siberian Ginseng.

Combinations Female Formula.

Synergistic Vitamins and Minerals Vitamin A (20,000 to 40,000 IU), B complex, Vitamin B_6 (25-100 mg), Vitamin B_1 (50 mg), PABA (up to 100 mg, a precursor for estrogen), Pantothenic acid (up to 100 mg, helps to delay menopause), Vitamin C (500 mg, three times daily), Vitamin E (800-1,200 IU) stimulates production of estrogen, Calcium/Magnesium (2 tablets, twice daily for rest of life).

Menstruation

Menstruation is the term for the discharge from the uterus of blood and other materials essential for pregnancy because fertilization has not occurred. Cramps, nervous tension, backache, water retention, menorrhagia (excessive or profuse flow), amenorrhea (suppressed or stopped flow) or dysmenorrhea (painful flow) are common menstrual difficulties.

Relief from Menstrual Cramps

On the inside of the leg, three finger widths up from the ankle bone is an acupressure point which, when stimulated forcefully for about five minutes will often relieve menstrual cramps.

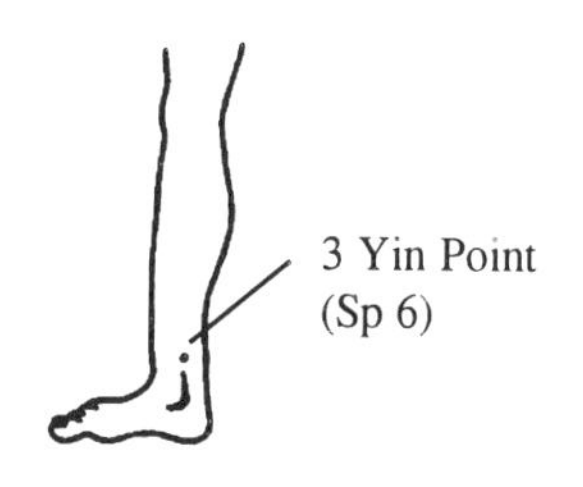

Recommended Action

Emmenagogue herbs stimulate and promote normal menstrual function and flow. If congestion from a recent cold is the cause of amenorrhea or dysmenorrhea, a good diaphoretic may be all that is necessary to relieve the problem. Tonics should be used in addition to stimulating diaphoretics if systemic or specific (organ) weakness is the cause. Avoid the use of purgative and strong cathartic laxatives.

Diet can also be a major cause of menstrual difficulties and can therefore correct some problems. The diet should include whole grains, nuts and seeds (especially sprouted), fresh fruits and vegetables, almonds, buckwheat, millet, oats, sesame and sunflower seeds (rich in Vitamin E and B complex), blackstrap molasses, grapes, and red beets (rich in iron). Yogurt, miso, sauerkraut and other fermented foods which contain Vitamin B_{12} help to restore the normal menstrual function. Thyroid deficiency may be indicated by irregular or profuse menstruation (see "Thyroid"). Lack of calcium and magnesium is also a common major cause of cramps.

Single Herbs Dong Quai, Ginger, White Oak Bark, Yarrow (orally or as a douche, for menorrhagia); Goldenseal, Black Cohosh, Blue Cohosh, Chamomile, St. John's Wort (amenorrhea); Ginger, Pennyroyal, Squaw Vine (dysmenorrhea).

Combinations Female Formula, Goldenseal Plus Formula.

Synergistic Vitamins and Minerals B complex, Vitamin B_6 (50-250 mg), Vitamin C (500-3000 mg daily), Multiminerals, Calcium (500 mg daily), Magnesium (250 mg daily), Mag. Phos. 6X tissue salt.

Suggested Program

Female Formula (2 capsules, three times daily), Beta-CEZB$_6$ (2 tablets, twice daily).

Migraine

(see also Headaches)

Migraines often start with some form of nausea, with a very painful throbbing headache, usually centered behind the eye. Often there are warning signs of auras, blurring of vision with bright spots in the vision. Migraines affect 15-20% of men and 25-30% of women. Often digestive problems are related, as migraines often affect the Gallbladder acupuncture areas. Food or environmental sensitivities, stress, and hormonal problems are often the cause of migraine. Toxins, Candida, a sluggish liver and constipation should all be considered as possible causes.

Feverfew for Migraine

By far the most significant supplement for migraine is feverfew. It is very important that the feverfew be guaranteed potency. We suggest 0.5% parthenolides, as this is the active ingredient. Many feverfew plants have no parthenolides whatsoever, so potency guarantees in supplements are especially important. The active ingredient has to build up in the body, taking 3-45 days to start working. The average is about six days. A person is really taking feverfew today for a migraine next week. We normally start with feverfew (1,000 mg, twice daily) for one month. It can be usually lowered to 500 mg, twice daily for another month, then lowered yet again to 500 mg daily, by the third or fourth months. Acupuncture has also been very beneficial in this area.

Recommended Action

We usually start most migraine programs with a 12 day D-tox Diet (see Appendix). During this time we try to find out if there are any food sensitivities, Candida or digestive problems. We suggest the avoidance of acid forming foods, dairy, flour, sweets, MSG, nitrites, chocolate and citrus. Red wine can sometime cause migraine. Since platelet aggregation is a major factor in migraines, we usually suggest no shellfish and reduced amounts of red meat. Cold water fish, high in essential fatty acids can be quite beneficial here. Other essential fatty acids, as found in evening primrose or borage oils are usually advantageous.

Single Herbs Feverfew, Ginger, Cayenne, Garlic, Ginkgo, Valerian, Evening Primrose oil, Borage Oil.

Combinations Feverfew Plus Formula, Cayenne Plus Formula, Essential Fatty Acid Formula.

Synergistic Vitamins and Minerals Beta-CEZB$_6$ (2 tablets, twice daily), B complex, Niacin (200 mg, three times daily), Vitamin B$_6$ (50 mg, three times daily, Quercitin (500 mg daily), Calcium (2,000 mg daily), Magnesium (500-1000 mg, daily).

Suggested Program

Start with a 12 day D-tox Diet.

Breakfast Feverfew Plus Formula (1-2 capsules), Essential Fatty Acids (1,000-2,000 mg), Beta-CEZB$_6$ (2 tablets).
Lunch Ester C (1,000 mg)
Supper same as breakfast.

Mucus

Mucus (noun) is a thick fluid which lubricates and protects the surfaces of the mucous (adjective) membranes by which it is secreted. Most people are familiar with the presence of mucus in the passages of the upper respiratory tract, nose and throat, but it is also present throughout the gastrointestinal and urogenital tracts.

Phlegm is the term for mucus in the throat, chest and lungs. A certain amount of mucus is vital to the function of body systems, but excessive secretion clogs the system, leads to degenerative disease and provides a potential haven for germs (see Infection).

Mucusless Diet

Foods that are most likely to cause mucus in the system are dairy and flour. Other foods like highly processed food, and excessive red meat, might also contribute to mucus content. A mucusless diet consists of no dairy, flour or processed food. You can usually eat the whole grains but not the flours of the grain. This should be adopted strictly for 2 months. After this amount of time, dairy or flour can be introduced into the diet 1-2 times per week, if there is no food sensitivity to these products.

Recommended Action

A few days of juice fasting will help to clean out the excess mucus. Then adopt a diet low in mucus by cutting down on dairy products, refined carbohydrates and meats. Eat fresh fruits, vegetables and potassium (vegetable) broth to obtain that element. Expectorant herbs are also beneficial in expelling mucus from the respiratory tract.

Single Herbs Goldenseal root (controls quality and quantity of mucus), Elderberry Extract (potassium); Comfrey, Fenugreek, Licorice, Marshmallow, Mullein, Thyme (expectorants); Lobelia Extract (emetic expectorant: phlegm is expelled in vomiting).

Combinations Goldenseal Plus Formula, Cleansing Formula, Lung Formula, Stomach Formula, Lower Bowel Tonic.

Synergistic Vitamins and Minerals Beta-CEZB_6, Beta-carotene (20,000 IU, twice daily), Vitamin C (500 mg, six times daily), Multitissue salts.

Muscle strain or soreness

Soothing Liniment

A good liniment for sore muscles, bursitis, bruises, pulled muscles and the like can be made from equal parts of Arnica Tincture and Cayenne Tincture. To these a little birch oil can be added if available. Rub the liniment into the area and relax.

Overexertion, or working muscles harder or longer than they are accustomed to, is the most common cause of muscle strain or soreness. Lactic acid is a byproduct of the chemical release of energy, which builds up in the cells of the muscle causing soreness, fatigue and stiffness.

Recommended Action

Proper diet and adequate exercise will maintain muscle tone and prevent soreness in normal circumstances. Calcium and magnesium supplements help as they are essential to muscle function. Massage relaxes the muscle fibers and helps to move lactic acid out of the cells and is therefore excellent for soreness and stiffness. It is more effective if herbal liniments are used.

Single Herbs Siberian Ginseng, Kava Kava (relaxing); Arnica Tincture, Cayenne Tincture (liniment for pain and swelling); Wormwood, Witch Hazel, Lobelia Extract (liniments); Alfalfa, Dandelion Root (calcium and magnesium); Saffron (prevents excess buildup of lactic acid).

Combinations Muscle Relaxing Formula, Nerve Formula, Trauma Ointment, Inflammation Ointment.

Synergistic Vitamins and Minerals Beta-carotene (two 10,000 IU capsules, twice daily), B complex, Vitamin B_{15} (100 mg, twice daily), Calcium/Magnesium (500/250 mg daily), Multiminerals (two, twice daily).

Nausea

Nausea, which can be caused by vertigo, morning sickness, food poisoning, emotional disturbance, improper eating and bacterial infections (especially of the intestinal tract), refers to the sensation that one is about to vomit.

Recommended Action

Anti-emetic herbs will generally relieve nausea unless it is caused by an acute case of food poisoning or infection. The cause is often the presence of putrid or undigested matter in the stomach, in which case it is best to cleanse the stomach by using an emetic to induce vomiting. If the emetic is preceded by a stimulant such as cayenne, peppermint or elder, this will prevent undue strain on the body from the "upward purge".

Single Herbs Lobelia Extract (3-5 drops), Meadowsweet, Cloves, Catnip, Peppermint, Spearmint, Peach leaves, Ginger root tea, Red Raspberry leaves (anti-emetic).

Any one of the following, in large amounts, cause emesis (vomiting): Lobelia Extract, Cayenne, Bayberry, Blessed Thistle, Dry Mustard.

Combinations Acute: Curing Pills. Chronic: Stomach Formula, Digestive Enzymes, Goldenseal Plus Formula, Lower Bowel Tonic.

Synergistic Vitamins and Minerals Calcium/Magnesium (500/250 mg), Multitissue salts.

Nervous Disorders

Afflictions of the brain and spinal cord and problems in the peripheral nervous system are classed as nervous disorders. Included in this type of problem are sclerosis, hardening of the brain or spinal cord tissues and various types of palsy. Multiple sclerosis is related to the brain and spinal cord and involves little patches of hardened or deadened tissue. Depending on the body parts which are connected with the affected nervous tissue, vision, speech or other body functions may be impaired. Palsy is either temporary or permanent partial paralysis. In Bell's palsy, usually just one side of the face is affected. In cerebral palsy, brain damage, which usually occurs prior to or during birth, causes muscular coordination problems. In Parkinson's disease, also known as shaking palsy or paralysis agitans, certain cells in the brain's muscle coordination center deteriorate.

Recommended Action

In advanced cases of nerve disorder, often little can be done, but if nothing is tried little gain can be expected. To eliminate toxic wastes from damaged and degenerating nervous tissue, cleanse the bowel and the blood and adopt a diet low in mucus. Nervine and antispasmodic herbs are essential for regenerating and renewing the nervous system. Cayenne, which has antispasmodic qualities and is a powerful circulatory stimulant and nutritive tonic, has alone been known to resolve some cases of temporary paralysis. Calcium and magnesium, principal ingredients of the myelin sheath which surrounds the nerves and nerve cells, can be found in plentiful supply in alfalfa. A few drops of garlic oil followed by B and B Tincture drops in the ear, will be beneficial in helping to rebuild the motor nerve centers at the base of the brain. Oil of Evening Primrose can help to build the myelin sheath.

Single Herbs Evening Primrose Oil, Alfalfa, Cayenne (nerve nutrients); Black Cohosh, Blue Cohosh, Blue Vervain, Gotu Kola (specifics for the brain); Skullcap (specific for spinal cord); Kava Kava, Lobelia Extract, Hops, Valerian, Wood Betony (nervine tonics and antispasmodics).

Combinations Nerve Formula, Muscle Relaxing Formula, Cleansing Formula (cleansing), B and B tincture, Lower Bowel Tonic (constipation).

Synergistic Vitamins and Minerals B complex (two, twice daily), Vitamin C (500 mg, twice daily), Multiminerals (two, twice daily), Trace Minerals, Multitissue salts, Lecithin (1200 mg, twice daily).

Nervous Tension

Nervous tension is characterized by restlessness, mental and physical unrest, emotional agitation, tension or tightness of the nerves and muscles, or a state of non-specific nervous excitation. The muscle tension causes headaches, stomach upset, muscle soreness and strain especially in the neck and shoulder area. Nervous tension is not actually a disorder, but a neuromuscular reaction to anxiety, stress or emotional conflict (either conscious or unconscious). This condition requires much greater amounts of calcium, magnesium, B vitamins and other specific nutrients for the body. If these nutrients are leached out of the body by excessive consumption of sugar and refined carbohydrates or if they are lacking in the diet, they will be taken from other sources within the body. Consequently, blood vessels, bones and especially nerves and the nerve sheaths suffer in an attempt to satisfy the body's metabolic need for calcium.

Recommended Action

All refined sugars and starches should be eliminated from the diet. Supplement with organic calcium, magnesium, Vitamin C and B complex. Nervine herbs are good for rebuilding weakened and frayed nerves and nerve sheaths. Often Ener-Jazz is very useful to reduce stress.

Single Herbs Alfalfa, Wild Oats, Comfrey; Hops (sedative nervine); Valerian, Lobelia Extract, Black Cohosh, Blue Cohosh, Kava Kava (relaxant nervines).

Combinations Muscle Relaxing Formula, Nerve Formula.

Synergistic Vitamins and Minerals Beta-CEZB$_6$, Vitamin A (10,000 IU daily), B complex (two, twice daily), Vitamin C (500 mg, three times daily), Vitamin D (400 IU daily), Calcium/Magnesium (600/300 mg daily), Multiminerals, Trace minerals, raw adrenal gland (when tension is associated with stress).

Nervous Tension

There is hardly anyone who doesn't suffer from time to time with a little nervous tension in our modern world. Nervous tension can cause a multitude of other problems as well. The following is a program we gave Mr. M., who came in with a fairly severe case of "nerves" from business and domestic stresses. He was given one B complex (twice daily), Nerve Formula (3 capsules, twice daily) Ener-Jazz (1 tsp., twice daily), one Ester C (500 mg, four times daily), Calcium/Magnesium (four daily), and two Multiminerals (twice daily). He also eliminated as much of his stress as possible by working fewer hours, thus helping both the business and domestic problems, and by starting a relaxing hobby. Within three months the tensions were much less. In six months the supplements were cut in half. Two years later, Mr. M. takes one B complex daily and considers life 'clear sailing'.

Nosebleed

Nosebleed (clinically known as epistaxis) is a common problem and often results from physical injury, such as a blow to the nose. Excessive dryness, sudden change in atmospheric pressure, scratching with the fingernail or blowing the nose too forcefully can also cause injury to the nasal lining. High blood pressure, nasal polyps or tumors, a blood disorder or simply a calcium deficiency (leaves nasal blood vessels weak and susceptible to rupture) may be indicated by persistent or recurring nosebleeds.

Recommended Action

Usually drinking a teaspoon of cayenne in a glass of warm water will remedy a nosebleed. In severe cases, snuff goldenseal root powder or White oak bark tea up the nose. Their astringent and homeostatic properties suffice to stop the bleeding. Bayberry bark and White oak bark are astringents and should be taken into the nose daily for recurrent cases (especially where polyps are present). These will strengthen the blood vessels and tissues of the nasal passages. Either use them as a tea and inhale through the nose or spray them in with an atomizer; or by using a straw, carefully inhale a very small amount of powder up the nose. Taking a calcium supplement will help to strengthen the nasal blood vessels.

Single Herbs Cayenne (vulnerary, hemostatic); Goldenseal root, White Oak bark, Barberry bark, Yarrow (hemostatic and astringent).

Synergistic Vitamins and Minerals Vitamin C (500 mg, four to six times daily), Bioflavonoids (1000-2000 mg daily), Calcium/ Magnesium (500/250 mg daily), Multivitamins and minerals (one, twice daily).

Obesity

See Weight Control.

Osteoporosis

The gradual loss of bone mass caused by the loss of bone minerals (especially calcium) and other bone components is called osteoporosis. Even though most people feel osteoporosis is strictly a lack of calcium, it is much more complex. This bone loss can cause fractures, especially in the hips and spinal vertebrae. This often results in loss of height, "dowager's hump" and spinal pain. Thinning can happen in both male and females, but is most common in postmenopausal women. Even though postmenopausal women have the highest incidence of osteoporosis, the lack of pre-menopausal female hormones is by no means the most important cause. Lack of load-bearing exercise, lack of an intake of proper nutrients, poor digestion and excessive excretion of bone nutrients ... all are stronger contributing factors.

Osteoporosis and Dairy ... a No-No

As a result of marketing, most people feel that the best thing for osteoporosis is to consume lots of dairy products. Why are we the only mammal that consumes dairy after being weaned? More than 90% of the adult population of the world doesn't consume dairy (only societies with strong marketing programs). Even though there is lots of calcium in dairy products, it is in a form that is hard to absorb. Because dairy can produce mucus in many people, it often inhibits the absorption of calcium from other sources. Their is plenty of calcium in meat, grains and many vegetables. Of course you can always take a supplement, if calcium is a problem.

Recommended Action

There is a lower incidence of osteoporosis in vegetarians than omnivores. It is interesting to note that there is no difference in bone mass up to the fifth decade. It appears that omnivores don't have a lower level of bone mass going into the risk time, but vegetarians lose less bone after the fifth decade. Adopting a vegetarian (or semi-vegetarian) diet part way through the fourth to fifth decade, seems therefore to be helpful. Both high protein and high sugar content in the diet increases calcium excretion, so consumption of both of these should be lowered.

A whole foods diet with a variety of fruits and vegetables and lots of whole grains appears very beneficial in lowering the incidence of osteoporosis. Foods high in proanthocyanidins and anthocyanidins (flavonoids with deep red-blue color) also have a positive effect. They can be found in many berries including hawthorn berries, blackberries, blueberries, cherries, and raspberries. They will help build up the bone matrix. Smoking, caffeine and alcohol consumption have a negative effect on calcium balances and therefore are a "no-no" for osteoporosis. As mentioned above, moderate physical exercise seems to be the number one factor for reducing osteoporosis.

Single Herbs Dong Quai, Licorice, Unicorn Root, Black Cohosh, False Unicorn, Horsetail Grass, Comfrey, Oatstraw.

Combinations Female Formula, Vegetable Silica Formula.

Synergistic Vitamins and Minerals B complex (1 tablet, twice daily), Folic acid (1 mg daily), Vitamin B_6 (100 mg daily), Vitamin B_{12} (1 mg daily), Ester C (2,000-3,000 mg daily), Calcium Citrate (1,000-2,000 mg daily), Magnesium (500 mg daily), Boron (3 mg daily), Hydroapetite (special form of calcium).

Suggested Program

Breakfast Female Formula (2 capsules), Vegetable Silica Formula (2 capsules), Digestive Enzymes (1-3 capsules with other supplements), Ester C (1,000 mg), B complex (1 tablet), Calcium/Magnesium (2 tablets).

Lunch Ester C (1,000 mg), Calcium/Magnesium (2 tablets), Boron (3 mg daily), B complex (1 tablet, twice daily).

Supper same as breakfast

Pancreas

The pancreas, a small gland which lies behind the stomach, has a twofold purpose. It functions as part of the digestive system by secreting a powerful enzymatic juice through the pancreatic ducts into the small intestine. It also functions as part of the endocrine (ductless gland) system by secreting insulin and glucagon directly into the bloodstream. These substances regulate the body's use of glucose and therefore its blood sugar level. In diabetes mellitus (also called hyperglycemia) the body cells are unable to metabolize or use glucose due to the insufficiency or unavailability of insulin. Consequently, the glucose must remain in the bloodstream. In hyperglycemia (too much sugar in the blood) the body will try to eliminate some of this excess sugar through the kidneys. Normally they operate to prevent glucose from being lost in the urine. Water and salts are lost under this abnormal condition and it may lead to dehydration. If diabetes is severe and untreated, metabolizing fats and proteins instead of carbohydrates causes excessive amounts of keto acids (byproducts of fat metabolism) in the blood and urine. Hypoglycemia (not enough sugar in the blood) can involve the pancreas or the adrenal glands (see also Hypoglycemia). Treatment of the diabetic should only be done under the guidance of a health practitioner.

Recommended Action

To prevent dehydration, drink lots of steam-distilled or reverse osmosis water daily. This will also benefit the blood and urine. When drinking fruit juices ensure that each mouthful is swished around in the mouth for at least 15 seconds, to mix in the saliva well and break down the fruit sugars. Also fruits and vegetables should be well chewed and all concentrated or refined starches and sugars eliminated from the diet.

Single Herbs Cedar Berries (strengthens endocrine function), Fringetree Bark (strengthens digestive function).

Combinations Glucose Formula.

Synergistic Vitamins and Minerals B complex (two, twice daily), Vitamin C (500 mg, six times daily), Vitamin E (400 IU), Multivitamins and minerals (one, twice daily), zinc, chromium, lecithin, nucleic acid.

Parasites

Parasites (either plant or animal) are organisms that take their nourishment from the host in which (or on which) they are living. Pathogens are parasites which cause damage and disease. Viruses, bacteria, rickettsia, fungi and worms are all parasites affecting man. Most people are familiar with viral and bacterial infections (see Infection). Typhus Q and Rocky Mountain Spotted Fever, and Lyme disease are caused by rickettsia, transmitted by fleas and ticks. Fungal diseases are caused by moulds and yeasts. They do not produce chlorophyll and must get their food from other organic matter. Ringworm, athlete's foot, yeast infections, candidiasis of the skin, mouth and vagina are all superficial fungus infections; coccidioidomycosis ("Cocci") and histoplasmosis, which attack the organs of the body, are deep systemic-type fungal infections. Parasitic worms are roundworms (nematodes) including pinworms, hookworms and trichina (or flatworms including tapeworms and flukes). Parasites are the cause of a variety of symptoms, such as fever, chills, nausea, diarrhea, skin rashes, itching and breathing difficulties, and may be responsible for allergic reactions, lesions, abnormal growths and toxic reactions similar to poisoning. Nutritional loss, anemia, cell damage, trauma and obstructions in organs and body systems are caused particularly by worms, their presence being indicated by restlessness at night, excessive nose picking, grinding the teeth and rectal itching.

Recommended Action

Getting Rid of Those Worms

Parasites are everywhere. Dr. J. R. Christopher used to say that a small proportion of his patients over 45 years had parasites - 95%. The best herbs for parasites that we have found are wormwood and male fern root. We also suggest taking lots of garlic and pumpkin seeds in your diet. The best time to work on parasites is three days before the full moon until four days after the full moon. Many parasites lay their eggs at this time and are therefore the most vulnerable.

Although improper hygiene and sanitation habits are usually related to worms, internal uncleanliness is the major cause, since all parasites function essentially as scavengers in the overall ecological system. Virtually all parasitic organisms operate in the same way as germs, acting as "garbagemen" to clean up the environment. It is important to cleanse and tone the bowel, blood and liver, the bowels often being the first organ subject to parasitic attack. Enemas involving astringent and anthelmintic herbs are beneficial. Anthelmintic herbs are of two types - vermifuges (expel worms) and vermicides (destroy worms). Better results will be achieved if these are taken with a diet low in mucus and one including foods such as onions, garlic, pickles and large quantities of pumpkin seed, all of which are offensive to worms. Take two Parasite Formula, twice daily for a month, alternating with one month of acidophilus. Repeat this process three times or for up to six months.

Black walnut extract preceded by a few drops of garlic oil is a potent fungicide. (It is also a specific remedy for persistent yeast-related diaper rash). Since superficial fungus infections thrive on warm moisture, make sure that the area is kept cool and dry. Remember that parasites are everywhere and the only way to avoid them is through internal and external cleanliness. We have a natural internal barrier against parasites, being HCl in the stomach. Adequate acid formation in the stomach will destroy most parasites.

See also Candida.

Single Herbs Chamomile, Chaparral, Garlic, Peach Leaves, Male Fern, Wormwood, Black Walnut, Senna, Pumpkin Seeds (anthelmintic); Black Walnut Extract, Garlic (vermicide and fungicide).

Combinations Parasite Formula, Lower Bowel Tonic, Liver Formula.

Suggested Program

Parasite Formula (2 capsules, twice daily for a month). Stop for a month and repeat for a month 2 more times. During "off" months, take acidophilus (2 capsules, twice daily). The program should therefore last six months.

Pelvic Inflammatory Disease (PID)

See also Infections and Candida

This acute (sometimes developing into chronic) infection of the uterus and Fallopian tubes can recur over months for a period of several years. PID is often cause by untreated infections such as chlamydia. Intrauterine devices (IUDs) can often precipitate the problem.

Recommended Action

This is often a case where antibiotics are the best initial treatment. These would usually be pharmaceuticals but goldenseal root and coptis can also be very beneficial here. A whole food diet and proper balance of body flora are also important. After the acute stage is over, we usually start with a 12 day D-tox Diet to cleanse the digestive tract and normalize the liver.

Single Herbs Acute stage: Goldenseal, Gold Thread (Coptis), Barberry, Echinacea, Garlic, Chlorella. After: Dong Quai, Black Cohosh, Licorice, Echinacea.

Combinations Female Formula, Goldenseal Plus Formula, Echinacea Plus Formula.

Synergistic Vitamins and Minerals Beta-CEZB$_6$ (2 tablets, twice daily), Beta-carotene (20,000 - 50,000 IU, twice daily), B complex (1 tablet, twice daily), Vitamin C (up to 10 g throughout the day), Vitamin E (800 IU daily).

Periodontal Disease

Periodontal Problems and Minerals

Periodontal problems plague more people over 35 than any other disease. This can be traced back to their dietary habits. It has been shown in many studies that most periodontal problems can be aided with minerals, especially calcium, magnesium, and potassium. We suggest 1000 mg of both potassium and calcium daily with 500 mg of magnesium. A good multimineral is also necessary. As far as herbs go, we suggest chlorella. By taking chlorella powder and putting it in a Water Pik® and spraying it on the gums good results can be obtained. We have found good results with a paste made up of 3 parts chlorella, 2 parts oak bark, 1 part myrrh, and 1 part propolis. Opening a capsule of Vitamin E (400 IU) and rubbing it on the gum has also been useful. All are useful powders to place (against the gums) in the mouth before going to bed. The above very simple program has aided many people.

Periodontal means "located around a tooth", and may refer to any disorder of the gums or other supporting structures of the teeth. Gingivitis (inflammation of the gums) is the most common form of periodontal disease and is frequently a result of improper diet, ill-fitting dentures, uneven bite, plaque buildup or some other source of irritation. In necrotizing gingivitis (trench mouth) infection is the cause. Pyorrhea (parodontitis) is a condition resulting from the above if the inflamed gums (which are swollen and red, and bleed when brushed) are not cared for. It is characterized by receding gums, weakened tooth sockets and loose teeth. Thrush is a yeast infection of the mouth, characterized by creamy white patches coating the inside of the mouth, and is generally accompanied by a foul odor. If it gets into the bronchial tubes and lungs it can be fatal.

Recommended Action

Use organic calcium/magnesium supplements to strengthen the teeth and tooth sockets along with astringent herbs to tone and restore life to the gums.

Single Herbs Chlorella (apply paste on gums), Red Raspberry Leaf tea and White Oak Bark (applied between cheek and gums morning and night for all cases); Black Walnut extract (antibiotic and antifungal), for trench mouth and thrush, Goldenseal root.

Synergistic Vitamins and Minerals Beta-CEZB$_6$, Beta-carotene (20,000 IU), B complex (one, twice daily), Vitamin C (500 mg, six times daily), Vitamin D (800 IU daily), Calcium/Magnesium (600/300 mg), Potassium (600 mg), Multiminerals, Trace minerals.

Pituitary

The pituitary governs the other endocrine and reproductive glands in the system and is therefore often referred to as the "master gland" of the body. Metabolic processes (such as growth) and the maintenance of proper fluid levels in the body are also regulated by the pituitary gland. A multitude of problems such as abnormal growth patterns and disorders of the thyroid, adrenals, kidneys and reproductive organs can result from malfunction of the pituitary.

Single Herbs Chlorella, Alfalfa, Kelp, Ginseng, Gotu Kola, Fo-ti-teng, Chlorophyll.

Synergistic Vitamins and Minerals B complex, Choline, Niacin, Vitamin C (500 mg, six times daily), Multivitamins and minerals, Calcium (250 mg), Magnesium (500 mg), Raw Pituitary.

Premenstrual Syndrome (PMS)

This group of symptoms (syndrome) usually happens 7-14 days before menstruation begins. The symptoms may include: depression, cramps, water retention, skin eruptions, headaches, bloated abdomen, breast swelling and tenderness, backaches, nervousness, insomnia, mood swings, fatigue, joint pain, fainting spells, and often personality changes (such as violence, outbursts of anger or withdrawal). PMS can also coincide with a craving for sweets, salt, bowel disturbance, acne, headaches and memory impairment. PMS often has to do with hormonal problems but can also be linked to food sensitivities, candidiasis, or malnutrition. PMS can be subcategorized into four types, but is clinically treated almost the same, with slight variations. Also consider possible Candida problems.

Recommended Action

It is interesting to note that most women with PMS have significantly different dietary habits than symptom-free women. PMS women consume 62% more refined carbohydrates (mostly flour), 275% more refined sugar, 79% more dairy, 78% more sodium, 53% less iron, 77% less manganese, 53% less zinc. Women can respond greatly by just reducing the refined sugar in their diet, taking a multiple vitamin/mineral and Vitamin B_6. The single most important supplement is Vitamin B_6.

Single Herbs Dong Quai, Alfalfa, Licorice, Unicorn Root, Black Haw, Raspberry Leaves, Blessed Thistle, Black Cohosh, Evening Primrose or Borage Seed Oils.

Combinations Female Formula, Essential Fatty Acids.

Synergistic Vitamins and Minerals Beta-CEZB_6 (2 tablets, twice daily), Beta-carotene (20,000 IU, twice daily), B complex (1 tablet, twice daily), Vitamin B_6 (100-250 mg, one-three times daily), Vitamin C (3,000 mg daily), Vitamin E (200-400 IU daily), Magnesium aspartate (400-800 mg daily), Zinc (10-50 mg daily).

Suggested Program

Breakfast Female Formula (2-3 capsules), Essential Fatty Acids (2-3 capsules), Beta-CEZB_6 (2 tablets).
Lunch Ester C (1,000 mg), Vitamin B_6 (100 mg).
Supper same as morning

Prostate

Prostate and Saw Palmetto

As a man ages, the form of male hormones produced often changes. This new hormone does not eliminate itself from the prostate as easily and causes cell proliferation in the prostate. This enlarges the prostate and can be a precursor to more significant problems in the future. Saw palmetto has been shown to reverse this process, aiding in reducing the size of the prostate in as little as 30 days.

The most common problem of the male urogenital system relates to this gland, which is an accessory male sex organ. It is situated directly beneath the bladder and is shaped somewhat like a donut, it encircles the urethra (the urinary outlet). Its purpose is to contract and squeeze its fluid secretions (containing elements necessary to the semen) into the urethral tract during ejaculation. Prostatitis, or inflammation and enlargement, can partially or totally block the flow of urine out of the bladder, resulting in urine retention. This causes the bladder to become distended, weak and susceptible to infection as a result of the increased amount of bacteria in the retained urine. Infection is easily transmitted from the bladder up the ureters to the kidneys. Benign or cancerous tumors, the formation of stones (calculi), hardening (sclerosis) and congestion (from prolonged stimulation followed by suppression or incomplete ejaculation) can also afflict the prostate. Frequent and increased urination (especially at night), difficulty in urinating, lessening of the force of flow and an accompanying burning sensation are all symptoms of prostate problems.

Recommended Action

Incorporate raw seeds (especially pumpkin seeds), nuts and whole grains into the diet to obtain elements such as zinc and essential fatty acids (EFA, such as Evening Primrose oil, borage or flaxseed oil) which are important for prostate health. Raw pumpkin seeds eaten daily are helpful for almost all prostate troubles. Juice and distilled or reverse osmosis water should be taken in large amounts. In all cases, juice fasting is also very effective. All diuretic herbs, specifically parsley and buchu, have a tonic effect on the urogenital system and are helpful for this condition.

Single Herbs Saw Palmetto, Pygeum, Chaparral, Echinacea (cleansers, alterative tonics); Goldenseal (diuretic and antiseptic); Juniper Berries, Parsley, Uva Ursi, Buchu (diuretics and tonics for urinary tract); Ginseng (specific for male reproductive organs).

Combinations Men's Formula, Kidney Formula, Cranberry Concentrate Plus Formula.

Synergistic Vitamins and Minerals Vitamin A (20,000 IU), Vitamin B_6 (50 mg), Vitamin C (500 mg, three to six times daily), Vitamin E (400-1200 IU), Zinc (75 mg), Copper (15 mg), Multiminerals, Bee Pollen, Lecithin, Fish liver oil.

Suggested Program

Take Men's Formula (two, three times daily), Beta-$CEZB_6$ (2 tablets, twice daily), Eat a handful of pumpkin seeds daily and eat fish two-three times a week for three-six months.

Psoriasis

see Skin Problems

Rheumatic Fever

Streptococcus infections such as strep throat or scarlet fever precede rheumatic fever, which may affect the skin, bones and joints and causes symptoms resembling arthritis or other connective tissue disorders.

Sydenham's Chorea or St. Vitus' Dance (a spasmodic twitching of the body) occurs when the brain and spinal cord are affected. Even without these other symptoms it frequently causes carditis, an inflammation of the heart. This in turn can cause permanent damage (rheumatic heart disease) to the heart valves or to the muscles of the interior lining. Aching in different joints, abnormal rhythm of the heart, small lumps or nodules under the skin, rash, fatigue, fever, and loss of weight or appetite are all indicative of rheumatic fever.

Recommended Action

Juice fasting will cleanse the entire system, while Lower Bowel Tonic or garlic and/or a catnip enema will keep the bowels free and moving. The individual symptoms should be dealt with separately as indicated under nervous disorders, arthritis, heart problems, etc., taking care not to overwork the heart. There have been indications that the bioflavonoids (citrin, hesperidin, quercitin, rutin etc.) have an advantageous affect on rheumatic fever. (See also Fevers, Scarlet Fever). The Arthritis diet (in Appendix) should be adopted.

Scarlet Fever

Scarlet Fever, also known as "Scarlatina" (in its milder form), is an acute streptococcus infection. It usually begins with a sore throat, swollen lymph nodes and a phlegmatic cough and is indicated by a scarlet skin rash, particularly in the groin and armpits, and by a red coating on the tongue ("Strawberry tongue"). The rash begins to show when the infection has spread throughout the system and is frequently accompanied by fever, chills, vomiting and, in some cases, convulsions. The rash will clear and the other symptoms subside within a few days, but the body is left in a weakened condition and is susceptible to other bacterial infections or to further complications such as rheumatic fever or rheumatic heart disease. Care should therefore be taken to prevent further complications of the strep infection.

Recommended Action

Do a few days of juice fasting along with plenty of Lower Bowel Tonic or catnip or garlic enemas which will keep the bowels free and moving. Take copious amounts of liquid every hour, if possible, while taking saffron (especially in combination with catnip). This will help to bring out the rash and often has the added effect of bringing down the fever. To draw out the toxins use ginger baths and diaphoretic herbs and drink lots of fluids to replace those lost. Infection-fighting herbs should also be used to regulate this condition. As scarlet fever can be severe in some cases, destroying the kidneys and weakening the heart, a physician should be consulted. It is often more prudent to take an antibiotic to get over this problem easily and spend the next few months rebuilding the body from the effects of the antibiotic than it is to spend many years rebuilding a damaged heart or kidneys.

Single Herbs Catnip (for enemas, also orally as a diaphoretic and febrifuge); Garlic (for enemas, also orally as antibiotic); Saffron (diaphoretic, encourages break out of rash); Ginger, Yarrow, Blessed Thistle, Sage (diaphoretics); Goldenseal, Echinacea.

Combinations Lower Bowel Tonic (to keep bowel free and moving).

Nip Scarlet Fever in The Bud

Scarlet Fever in itself is not really a severe problem, but the complications that can arise from it are. It can do severe damage to both the heart and the kidneys. Scarlet Fever often affects young children whose parents have had strep throat. The parents, trying to follow a "Natural Way", often get confused and try to fix the strep throat with Vitamin C and Vitamin A which are not strong enough. If the strep throat is passed to the child, it is probable that scarlet fever will result in the child. If the parents would take antibiotics for their throat problem, spending the next one to three months cleaning up the side effects of the antibiotics, the results would be a lot better than spending years trying to fix the child's weakened kidneys or heart from the scarlet fever.

Sciatica

Sciatica is an irritation of the sciatic nerve, located in the lower back and radiating (partially or completely) down the leg to the foot. The problem usually starts in the lower back or muscle spasm along the nerve route.

Recommended Action

The most important thing is to find out if there is any injury, protruding vertebra disk, or trauma that might have caused the problem. Excessive stress (physical, emotional or sexual) can cause sciatica. We have found very good success with acupuncture for sciatica.

Single Herbs Kava Kava, Turmeric.

Combinations Muscle Relaxing Formula, Inflammation Ointment (rub on area).

Synergistic Vitamins and Minerals Ester C (1,000 mg, four times daily), Vitamin D (200-400 IU daily), Manganese (50 mg), Calcium (400-800 mg daily), Magnesium (400-800 mg daily). Intramuscular injection of Vitamin B_{12} (1,000 mcg) and Folic Acid (2-3 mg), two to three times a week.

Shingles

In this condition herpes zoster virus causes infection of the peripheral nerves of the body. Swelling of the lymph nodes, reddening of the skin and eruption of blisters are indications of shingles. The blisters are extremely sensitive to the touch and may itch or burn, but within a few weeks they dry up, crust over and finally drop off. There are usually no serious long-range effects unless the eyes become infected, in which case blindness may result. This condition is sometimes followed by temporary paralysis or neuralgia of the affected area. (See also Herpes).

Recommended Action

A three-day juice fast (or even 10 day Lemon Aid Cleanse) along with plenty of Lower Bowel Tonic will cleanse the system of toxins. Nervine herbs will soothe and strengthen the inflamed nerves, while calcium and magnesium supplements will help rebuild them. Apple cider vinegar diluted with water, used as often as necessary to bathe the affected areas of the skin, will give temporary relief.

Single Herbs Reishi, Licorice, Valerian, Hops (calm the nerves).

Combinations Reishi Plus Formula, Nerve Formula, Inflammation Ointment.

Shock

The trauma of serious injury, the sudden spread of severe infection, a great loss of blood, a serious allergic reaction, or a severe emotional trauma, may bring on shock. It is characterized by pale skin color and cold, moist skin. Other indications are dilated pupils, a vacant look, shallow and irregular breathing and a weak but fast pulse. During shock the protective reflexes and vital processes of the body (particularly the blood pressure and circulation) become dangerously depressed.

Shock is a fairly normal reaction to any dramatic situation, be it an accident, severe loss of blood or emotional trauma. In cases of shock always give 1/4 -1 tsp. of cayenne pepper in some water if the person is conscious. If unconscious, put a few drops of Bach Rescue Remedy on the lips. Get the person to sip a glass of water with a few drops of Rescue Remedy in it if conscious. Always keep the person warm.

Recommended Action

The most important measure to normalize blood pressure and circulation is to take 1/4 - one teaspoon of cayenne in a glass of warm water. Massaging lobelia extract into the abdominal area, the solar plexus, the neck and back of the head will relax the muscles and nerves, allowing freer circulation. Taking nervine herbs, either orally or as enemas, will relax the system even further and normalize vital processes.

Single Herbs Cayenne, Lobelia Extract, Hops, Skullcap, Valerian, Catnip.

Combinations Nerve Formula, Bach Rescue Remedy.

Sinus infection (Sinusitis)

See also Allergies, Cold and Flus, Infections, Lungs, Mucus.

Sinusitis is inflammation of the nasal sinuses (part of the upper respiratory system). Sinus problems can be caused by allergies, bacteria associated with viral infection (common cold), dental problems, or environmental issues. Sinus problems can often become more problematic when a person eats too much mucus forming foods.

Allergies and Sinus Problems

The most common cause of sinus problems is an allergy to dairy and/or flour. By adopting a mucusless diet and taking Beta-CEZB$_6$ (2 tablets, two times daily) and Lung Formula (3 capsules, 2-3 times daily), the problem can usually be relieved. After two-three months, a minor amount of these foods can often be consumed without a problem.

Recommended Action

A person with this problem has to adopt a mucusless diet and therefore not consume dairy or flour. We usually suggest a 12 day D-tox Diet (see Appendix) after the acute stage is over, if a person has recurring problems. If the mucus gets too thick, often drinking hot liquids like green tea, will be beneficial. Eating lots of raw food during the mucus stage can speed up recovery. Of course volatile oils, such as eucalyptus, mint etc. can be very helpful. Just rub these into your hand and inhale. They can also be applied to a humidifier or diffuser. Boil chamomile in a pot. Drape a towel tent over your head and breath the steam in through your nose. It can do wonders.

Single Herbs Goldenseal Root, Garlic, Echinacea, Chamomile, Linden Flowers, Menthol, Eucalyptus oils.

Combinations Goldenseal Plus Formula, Lung Formula, Echinacea Plus Formula.

Synergistic Vitamins and Minerals Beta-CEZB$_6$ (2-3 tablets, 2-3 times daily), Beta-carotene (100,000 IU, twice daily), Vitamin C (500-1,000 mg every two hours), Bioflavonoids (1,000 mg daily), Zinc (20-60 mg daily).

Suggested Program

Breakfast Lung Formula (2-3 capsules), Beta-CEZB$_6$ (2-3 tablets), Goldenseal Plus Formula (2 capsules), Beta-carotene (an extra 20,000-30,000 IU).

Lunch Lung Formula (2-3 capsules), Beta-CEZB$_6$ (2-3 tablets).

Supper Lung Formula (2-3 capsules), Beta-CEZB$_6$ (2-3 tablets), Goldenseal Plus Formula (2 capsules), Beta-carotene (an extra 20,000-30,000 IU, twice daily).

Ester C (1,000 mg, every two hours). Adopt a mucusless diet. Use the Chamomile steam tent and/or volatile oils several times daily.

Skin Problems

Acne (dealt with elsewhere), eczema and psoriasis are common skin problems. Eczema is characterized by blistered or crusted and scaling lesions which are almost always accompanied by severe itching. In this case secondary infection can be a problem, especially if the top layers of skin have been destroyed by scratching. Psoriasis (often a persistent and chronic problem which can last a lifetime) is characterized by pink or red patches covered with silvery scales and rarely produces pain or itching. A breakdown in the function of the skin as an eliminative organ is indicated in all skin disorders. The skin plays a major part in excreting wastes resulting from body processes and is therefore often referred to as the "third kidney" or "third lung". Poor bathing habits, using soaps that clog the pores, wearing synthetic materials which don't "breathe" and eating foods which produce excessive amounts of mucus and toxic wastes, all prevent proper functioning of the skin. When any area of the skin ceases to function properly, a greater burden is placed upon the remainder which still functions effectively, resulting in congestion and deterioration as toxic wastes attempt to escape through a limited area of skin surface.

Recommended Action

A juice fast and a diet low in mucus along with herbs for the bowel and blood will cleanse the body of mucus and toxic waste. Skin irritation can be relieved by using chickweed in the form of a fomentation or ointment, while apple cider vinegar or Yellow dock tea applied externally will relieve itching.

Aloe vera gel may be taken internally or externally to relieve skin irritation. Black walnut extract, or a poultice or Bone, Flesh and Cartilage fomentation, is also beneficial. We have also had success with Inflammation Ointment in some cases. The best herb found for skin problems is oil of evening primrose.

Single Herbs Chickweed/Chickweed Ointment, Chamomile Ointment, Essential fatty acids (such as are contained in Evening Primrose Oil, Borage etc.), Aloe Vera, Black Walnut Extract (specifics for skin); Echinacea, Burdock, Dandelion Root (blood cleansers), Oil of Evening Primrose (builder).

Combinations Cleansing Formula, Lower Bowel Tonic, Reishi Plus Formula, Bone, Flesh and Cartilage, Inflammation Ointment.

Synergistic Vitamins and Minerals Vitamin A (20,000 IU), B complex (two, twice daily), Niacin (125 mg, twice daily), Vitamin C (three 500 mg, six times daily), Multivitamins and minerals.

Sore Throat

see also Sinus, Cold/flu, Infection.

A sore throat is usually an extension of some other problem. It can often be related to a sinus problem, cold, flu, allergies or viral infection. If you have a very sore red throat for extended period of time, it could be a strep throat. In this case, it is often best to get antibiotics. The complications that strep throat can cause are more severe than the side effects of antibiotics.

Recommended Action

It is important to adopt a mucusless diet. Take antibiotics if needed. Make sure you take Acidophilus while taking the antibiotics and for at least one month after.

Single Herbs Goldenseal, Echinacea (tincture best), Garlic, Slippery Elm (lozenges).

Combinations Echinacea/Goldenseal Tincture (1 tsp., every two hours), Echinacea Plus Formula, Goldenseal Plus Formula.

Synergistic Vitamins and Minerals Beta-CEZB$_6$ (2-3 tablets, 2-3 times daily), Beta-carotene (30,000 IU, two times daily), Vitamin C (1,000 mg, every two hours), Zinc lozenges (1 every two hours).

Sprains, Strain and Athletic Injuries

Whiplash, torn ligaments, joint instability, stressed muscles, stretched ligaments are all common ailments to do with the skeletal muscular system. Everyone runs across at least one of these problems.

Recommended Action

Usually the first thing to do is put ice on the area. Frozen peas or corn often works the best, as they will form to the shape of the injured area and can be easily re-frozen. We usually apply Trauma Ointment as soon as possible to soothe the area. It can be reapplied as often as desired. If inflammation seems to be present, the Inflammation Ointment can be added.

Single Herbs Bromelain and Curcumin, Kava Kava.

Combinations Muscle Relaxing Formula, Trauma Ointment, Inflammation Ointment.

Synergistic Vitamins and Minerals Vitamin C (3,000 mg throughout the day), Bioflavonoids (up to 1,000 mg daily), Manganese (50 mg), Zinc (30 mg daily), Multiminerals, Glucosamine Sulphate (up to 1,500 mg daily).

Tendonitis

Tendons are the elastic fibers that connect muscles to bones. When they become inflamed, usually as a result of injury or sometimes infection, the condition is known as tendonitis. Weakness of a particular muscle and specific pain associated with any movement of the muscle are indicative of tendonitis. Calcium deposits around the tendons and synovial bursa of the shoulder create a condition known as calcific tendonitis or bursitis.

> **Tendonitis**
>
> Tendonitis occurs very often in musicians and athletes. The best thing we have found for this is Dr. Christopher's formula "Bone, Flesh and Cartilage". You make a fomentation out of this and apply it hot at least once daily. This product is also available in ointment form which can be applied topically. The accompanying vitamins should be taken with the Muscle Relaxing Formula and Calcium Pangamate (N,N-dimethylglycine, 100 mg, twice daily), Vitamin B_6 (250 mg, twice daily), and Trauma Ointment.

Recommended Action

It is important first of all to locate and remove the source of the inflammation. Bone, Flesh and Cartilage combination used both internally and externally will not only help to heal the injury but will also relieve the inflammation in the tendon. Massaging Trauma Ointment or lobelia extract into the affected area will give some relief from pain.

Single Herbs Comfrey (cell proliferant, heals damaged tissues); Cayenne/Arnica Tinctures (equal parts as a liniment).

Combinations Muscle Relaxing Formula, Nerve Formula, B and B Tincture, Bone, Flesh and Cartilage, Trauma Ointment and Inflammation Ointment.

Synergistic Vitamins and Minerals Vitamin A (10,000 IU), B complex, Vitamin C (500 mg, three times daily), Multiminerals, Calcium/Magnesium (600/300 mg), Potassium (300 mg), trace minerals.

Thyroid

The thyroid (a butterfly-shaped gland located just below the Adam's apple in front of the trachea or windpipe) regulates many important body processes. It combines iodine compounds in the blood with certain amino acids to secrete hormones. Basal metabolism (rate of chemical processes such as changing food into energy and building proteins), growth, thought processes, maintenance of body fluid balance, blood cholesterol levels and adequate functioning of other endocrine glands are some of the body processes which the thyroid affects. Sluggishness, absentmindedness, nervousness, weight gain and chronic fatigue indicate an underactive thyroid (hypothyroidism), while increased metabolic rate, nervousness, restlessness, weight loss and a constant feeling of being too hot and sweating indicate an overactive thyroid (hyperthyroidism). Goiter (an abnormal enlargement of the thyroid gland) is a symptom of either one of these conditions.

Single Herbs Kelp, Dulse (specific tonics for thyroid); Mullein (specific for entire glandular system including thyroid); Alfalfa (specific for pituitary which regulates the thyroid); Garlic, Cayenne (antiatherosclerotics, assist cholesterol function of thyroid); Parsley (diuretic assists body fluid balance function of thyroid).

Tonsillitis

The tonsils (located on either side of the inner throat, behind the tongue) work together with the pharyngeal tonsil (located in the nasopharynx or upper part of the throat) to form the body's front line of defense against airborne bacteria entering the body through the mouth and nose. They are part of the lymphatic system, and when they become inflamed, from fighting infection, the condition is known as tonsillitis.

Recommended Action

Acute tonsillitis (a sudden bacterial invasion of the nose and throat) can be remedied by a three-day juice fast along with herbs that cleanse and strengthen the glandular system and those that keep the bowel free and moving. A toxic condition that the lymphatic system is unable to throw off is indicated in chronic tonsillitis, and long-term measures are necessary to clean and tone the bowel, the blood and the lymphatic system. In the abscessed condition known as quinsy, gargling with an astringent as well as a tea made of three parts mullein, one part lobelia (1 tsp of combined herbs in a cup of boiled water) may be an urgent necessity along with the same treatment as indicated for chronic tonsillitis. You have to be patient with tonsillitis and get plenty of bed rest.

Single Herbs Goldenseal, Echinacea (infection fighters); Mullein (specific for glandular system); Bayberry (astringent gargle).

Combination Goldenseal Plus Formula.

Synergistic Vitamins and Minerals Beta-carotene (30,000 IU, twice daily), Vitamin C (500 mg, six times daily).

Ulcers

Ulcers, as they are commonly known, refer to the peptic or gastric (stomach) and duodenal (upper intestine) variety, although they may appear on almost any part of the body, such as bed sores, which are called decubitus ulcers. A craterlike lesion is left on the surface of the skin or mucous membrane when dead tissue sloughs off as a result of localized necrosis (tissue death). Gastric juices eat away the lining of the stomach or duodenum causing bleeding in severe situations. This can result in shock, anemia and other complications. A perforated ulcer occurs when the juices eat right through the mucous membrane. Severe inflammation of the peritoneal membrane lining the abdominal cavity may result, accompanied by a substantial amount of persistent pain and often nausea and vomiting.

Mucus and Ulcers

We have had great results with ulcers doing just the opposite of the allopaths. We strongly suggest **no** dairy or flour products. Adopt the Inner Cleanse diet for two weeks, pureeing food if necessary. Take Fare You (as directed on package). After two weeks remain on the diet but take one Stomach Tonic in the middle of meals.

Recommended Action

Eat smaller but more frequent meals (six to eight light meals daily) to reduce the amount of gastric juices necessary. Thoroughly chewing and salivating each bite will enhance digestion and remove much of the burden from the gastric juices. Unless raw fruits and vegetables are soft, bland kinds (such as avocados, bananas and squash). They should be blended, pureed or juiced until recovery is well under way. Avoid citrus and other highly acid fruits for some time and eliminate all fried foods and refined carbohydrates. A specific remedy for duodenal ulcers is raw, freshly made, cabbage juice, while stomach ulcers respond well to raw, freshly made, potato juice. It is important that these remedies be made fresh each time. They may be taken individually, mixed together, or mixed with carrot or celery juices. Drink all liquids (juice, tea and even water) at a temperature as close as possible to that of the body. Cabbage juice often stings the first few times it is taken. A low mucus diet should be adopted. Even though a popular cure for ulcers is to drink plenty of milk, we feel that this will only aggravate the situation in the long run. We have been using a lot of a Chinese patent medicine called "Fare You" - formerly called "Vitamin U". This product is an extract of cabbage roots and works very effectively.

Single Herbs Licorice (especially deglycerrhized), Comfrey (pyrrolizidine alkaloid (PA)-free; demulcent and cell proliferant), Slippery Elm (soothing and nourishing).

Combinations Stomach Tonic, Fare You, Wei Te Ling.

Synergistic Vitamins and Minerals Calcium/Magnesium (250/125 mg before meals).

Urinary Tract Infection

see Bladder Infection.

Vaginal Problems

There are a multitude of vaginal problems such as tumors, cysts, polyps, strictures (narrowing or tightening of the tissues), fistulas (abnormal openings from or into another part of the body as a result of injury or infection), hernias (protrusions into the vagina by other organs or tissues) and uterine prolapse. Constitutional weakness in the female reproductive organs and supporting structures, which can be complicated by various other factors, is the basic cause of all these problems.

Recommended Action

Emmenagogue herbs have a tonic effect on the muscles and organs of the reproductive area and in combination with other astringent and tissue building herbs can achieve good results in rebuilding and strengthening these tissues. For simple yeast infections the best thing is a vaginal suppository of Homeopathic Candida, pulsatilla and acidophilus.

Combinations Female Formula, Vaginal Suppository.

Varicose Veins

Varicose veins usually occur as a result of the valves inside the veins (which normally prevent downward backflow) becoming weakened and failing in their function. This allows blood to fall back down the venous structure opposite to the normal flow, creating enlarged, twisted and swollen veins. They are commonly found on the legs of older people, pregnant women and those whose occupations require a lot of standing. People who do more walking, or other exercise, are not affected as often because muscular contractions squeeze against the veins to force the blood back up during exercise. The typical blue varicose veins seen on the surface of the legs are veins which have dilated or expanded as a result of the outward pressure on their walls as abnormal amounts of blood collect in them. The blue color is due to the lack of oxygen in venous blood, which is returning to the heart. Varicosity further disables the valves in the veins, and the situation therefore compounds itself and the veins become grossly distorted along with aching, cramping and general weakness. If sores and ulcers develop, they may be prevented from healing due to inadequate circulation. Thrombophlebitis (severe inflammation of the blood vessels, complicated by blood clots) is a dangerous condition that may then result.

Recommended Action

Much of the weakness of the valves and walls of the veins can be attributed to calcium deficiency, and it should therefore be taken as a supplement. White oak bark taken as a tea (simmered down to 1/4 its original amount) or applied as a fomentation is a specific astringent tonic for varicose veins. It can also be painted on like shellac and wrapped with a bandage as well as taken orally.

Single Herbs White Oak Bark, Collinsonia root, Witch Hazel.

Combinations Cleansing Formula.

Synergistic Vitamins and Minerals Bioflavonoids (1000 mg, three-six times daily), Rutin (500 mg, twice daily), Hesperidin (1500 mg, twice daily), Calcium, Multiminerals, Trace minerals.

Warts

Warts can be found virtually anywhere on the body. The most common places are hands, feet, forearms and face. They are raised solid growths on the skin and are usually painless. They are caused by viruses and can be contagious.

Recommended Action

Since warts are viral in nature, improving the immune system will help a lot. There are many folk remedies for warts. The one that I have found to be the most successful is the white latex found in the stems of dandelions. Apply fresh latex of a dandelion on the wart, three times a day for 7-10 days. The wart will turn dark and fall off. This method has been more than 90% effective. The only problem is it can only be done in dandelion season. Other methods that have worked are taking the peel of a black banana (old bananas) and apply the inside of the skin on the wart for one hour daily for a week. This method seems to be about 60% effective. Applying garlic or garlic oil on the wart sometimes works as does tincture of Lomatium. Applying a Vitamin C paste or liquid Vitamin A has sometimes been successful.

Single Herbs Dandelion latex, banana peels, garlic, Lomatium.

Combinations Echinacea Plus Formula.

Synergistic Vitamins and Minerals Beta-CEZB$_6$ (2-3 tablets, three times daily), Vitamin A (30,000-100,000 IU), Vitamin C (4,000-10,000 mg over a day), Zinc (50-80 mg daily).

Weight Control

Our modern diet and lifestyle makes it virtually impossible for some to maintain a normal, healthy body weight. Consequently, weight control has become an obsession in our society, but ideally this must include other factors related to optimum health such as exercise, rest, anxiety and stress, boredom, frustration and psychological hunger. Often nutritional deficiencies, metabolic abnormalities and in some cases glandular disorders must first be remedied before weight can be controlled effectively. If parasites are the cause of a voracious appetite, as is often the case, they must be eliminated first. Adopt a diet low in mucus and do periodic juice fasting as well as supplementing with such herbs as are indicated for the specific condition in all the above situations.

Citrimax® and weight loss

Citrimax®, a concentrate of *Garcinia cambogia*, is very good for weight loss. The major ingredient is Hydroxycitric acid (HCA). It will help inhibit the appetite and stop the formation of fat from the consumption of carbohydrates. We have seen people lose between 2-7 pounds a week by taking 2-3 capsules of Citrimax®, 30-90 minutes before each meal. After about 3-4 weeks, they will often plateau in weight loss. By continuing to take Citrimax®, after 2-4 weeks, weight loss will start again. The product is continued until the person reaches desired weight and maintains it for 3-4 weeks. Starting a weight loss program with a 12 day D-tox Diet obtains the best results.

Recommended Action

There are so many diet plans on the market that it is ridiculous. We have listed what we consider the best program in the Appendix along with the other diets. The reason we feel that the Ultimate Weight Loss Program is best is that it considers the metabolic function of the body. This program "tricks" the body into thinking it is fasting but at the same time keeps the metabolism high, thus burning off fat. (Refer to Ultimate Weight Loss Diet in Appendix.)

Single Herbs *Garcinia cambogia*, Oil of Evening Primrose, Chickweed, Glucomannan.

Combinations Psyllax, Citrimax® (*Garcinia cambogia*).

Synergistic Vitamins and Minerals Protein powder (predigested if possible), Multivitamins and minerals.

Yeast Infection

(see Candida, Vaginal Problems)

Appendix

Allergy Testing through Applied Kinesiology

There are many kinesiology tests that can be used to detect allergies. I use two different types depending on the strength of the person. By testing the strength of various muscles while a person is holding a certain food, cosmetic, cleaning detergent etc. you can often tell if an allergy may be present.

I usually use the shoulder muscle or the finger muscle to test a person for allergies. To start with I test the normal strength of their muscle, as shown in the diagrams. I then get the person to hold the substance being tested in the other hand, close to their stomach if it is considered a 'food'. If the substance is an environmental one, I have the person hold it at half an arm's-length from the body. If the substance has a tendency to cause an allergic reaction it will weaken the muscle tested in either case.

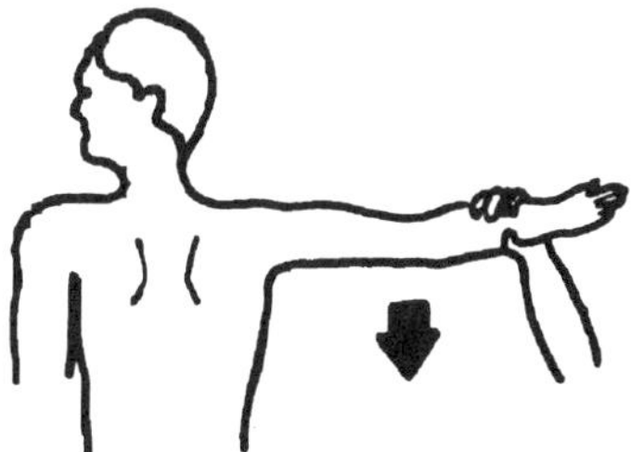

allergy testing through shoulder muscles

The first few times I did this I couldn't believe it worked, but "the proof of the pudding is in the eating", and after using this method for several years I find it quite accurate. The drawback of this method over the Pulse Test (see next page) is that it only tests the food or substance in its current state. The Pulse Test, however, tests the substance in its state after the body interacts with it. For example a person might not be allergic to potatoes, but due to a poor digestive system, may be allergic to half digested potatoes. The Pulse Test will show this whereas the Kinesiology Test will not.

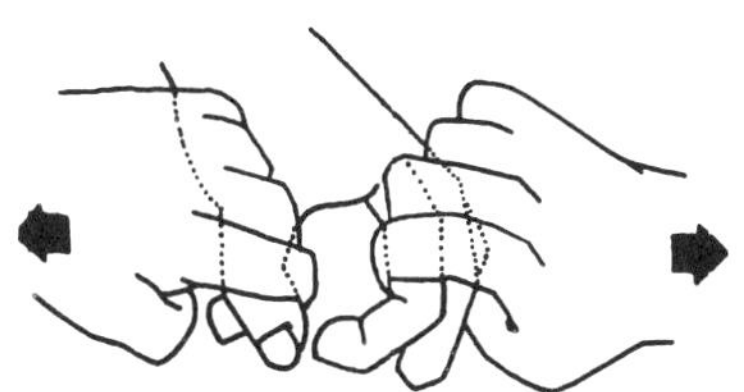

allergy testing through finger muscles

Coca's Pulse/Allergy Test

The Pulse Test is another way to test your allergies. It has been noted that the first indication of an allergy is a rise in a person's pulse. By keeping very close watch over the pulse while challenging different foods we can often determine possible allergies. By avoiding foods that cause an increased pulse rate we can aid in clearing allergies and can increase the general health of the person. There are six points to the pulse test.

1. Stop smoking, at least for the duration of the testing. Upon challenging cigarettes, they raise the pulse.

2. Take the pulse (usually on the wrist) for **one whole minute**, (not for 1/4 minute and multiplying it by 4, as done in the hospitals) at the following times.

   a) before rising (before sitting up in bed upon waking)
   b) before meals
   c) three times after each meal, at half hour intervals before retiring for the day

3. Record all foods eaten.

4. Repeat steps 2 and 3 for 2 - 4 days.

5. Do a single food challenge for two or more days. You do this by eating a small portion of a different food every hour, starting early in the morning and continuing for 12 -14 hours. Take your pulse just before eating the food and one-half hour after.

6. Over the day we have a normal range, one which differs from individual to individual. Any food that seems to elevate the pulse by six (6) points or more should be avoided. These foods should be challenged at other times to see if you get the same results.

Many allergies involve other than food substances, thereby making the data hard to interpret and resulting in frustration. Some foods do not cause a reaction unless eaten for more than three days in a row. Some allergies do not show up for two or more days after the food is eaten.

The charts on the next page will make the task of recording your pulse tests easier.

For more information consult *The Pulse Test* by A.F. Coca M.D., published by Arco Publishing Company, New York, N.Y.

Chart to test Food Allergies

	Day 1 Pulse	Day 2 Pulse	Day 3 Pulse	Day 4 Pulse
Before Rising				
Breakfast Diet 30 min 60 min 90 min				
Lunch Diet 30 min 60 min 90 min				
Dinner Diet 30 min 60 min 90 min				

Single Food Challenge

	Day 1 Pulse	Day 2 Pulse	Day 3 Pulse	Day 4 Pulse
food 30 min.				
food 30 min.				
food 30 min.				
food 30 min.				
food 30 min.				
food 30 min.				
food 30 min.				
food 30 min.				
food 30 min.				
food 30 min.				
food 30 min.				

Arthritis and Rheumatism Diet

- No refined grains, sugars, pasta
- No salt, baked goods, breads, or processed cereals
- No foods containing preservatives
- No coffee, black tea
- Limited red meats, sweets, dairy products, alcohol
- Less than 20% acid-forming foods (see chart in D-Tox Diet section)
- lots of raw food

One tablespoon Cod Liver Oil taken straight or in two tablespoons of orange juice or milk, thoroughly shaken, one hour before breakfast. Nothing else to be taken before breakfast.

Breakfast One tablespoon apple cider vinegar and 1/2 tablespoon Unpasteurized honey in 1/2 cup warm water. Fruit meal - a little yogurt can be added. It is preferred to have one type of fruit only, e.g. a bowl of cherries and yogurt, or a grape-fruit.

Supplements 2 Calcium/Magnesium
2 Multiminerals
2 Arthritis Formula

Morning Snack (if desired) Piece of fruit or vegetable, e.g. carrot sticks or celery or vegetable broth; cottage cheese or yogurt plus 500 mg Vitamin C (Vitamin C compulsory).

Lunch Major part of meal should be a green salad. Soup or a vegetable can also be eaten.

Supplements Ester C 500 mg
1 Tablespoon Aloe Vera
2 Arthritis Formula
400 IU Vitamin E

Afternoon Snack Similar to morning snack.

Supper Big salad, variety of cooked vegetables, a casserole, grain(preferably millet or buckwheat); a little meat can be eaten if desired.

Supplements Same as for breakfast

Evening Snack Same as morning snack.

Candida Diet

This following program has been very successful in combatting Candida (yeast) colonization. The program should last for 3-9 months, unless otherwise advised by a health practitioner. This program has to be adhered to more strictly than most, as "cheating" will only create a stronger strain of Candida in your body.

There are three basic components to the program:

1. Eliminating the foods that Candida lives on. This is the hardest yet most important part.
2. Inhibiting Candida with specific vitamins and destroying them with homeopathic remedies.
3. Strengthening the body so that Candida will not return.

Food and Drinks to be avoided

- All flour products (for 1 - 2 months)
- All dairy products (for 1 - 2 months; butter is alright)
- Any flour product with yeast (entire length of the program)
- Any curded or fermented dairy (after 1 1/2 months, yogurt is alright)
- All yeast or yeast-containing foods
- No peanuts, grapes, oranges, mushrooms, tropical fruits or melons
- No wine, beer, or vinegar (including sauces with vinegar; after 2 months vinegar is alright)
- No soya sauce, miso, tofu (after 1 1/2 months, these are alright)
- No sugar, or sweetening agents of any type
- No dried fruit
- No tea (herbal teas, including green tea, are alright)
- Only 1 piece of fruit daily, two cups of coffee (max), two ounces of distilled alcohol a week (if desired)

Good Foods

At first this might appear to leave very little to eat. Much of this feeling is due to cravings which you have had all along. On this program you can eat the following good foods:

- All the vegetables desired (except mushrooms)
- Meat (if desired; chicken and fish are best)
- Grains (flours of the grain are not alright, but the whole grains themselves are)
- Beans (not more than three times a week)
- Some fruit (apples, peaches, pears, plums, and berries; no more than the mass of an average sized apple daily)

Supplements

Homeopathic Candida 30X (5-10 drops, four times daily)
Beta-CEZB$_6$ (2 tablets, twice daily)
Digestive Enzymes (1-3 capsules with each meal)

After 1 1/2 months, add a high potency Acidophilus (2 capsules, twice daily)

Candida Long Questionnaire

This is the long questionnaire designed for adults and isn't appropriate for children. It is based on a questionnaire created by William G. Crook M.D. and his book *The Yeast Connection*. Modifications have been made to suit our clientele. It is appropriate to fill this questionnaire out every two years or so to check if the risk factors or symptoms related to Candida have increased enough to consider it an issue. There is a shorter questionnaire also. It helps keeps track of your symptoms on an ongoing basis. It can tell you when you are finished with the Candida problem.

This questionnaire lists factors in your medical history which can promote the growth of *Candida albicans* (Section I) and symptoms commonly found in people that have a Candida problem (Sections II and III). If the question applies in Section I, circle the number and add the score. In Sections II and III you are asked to rate symptoms. By adding all these numbers together we can see a probability of having a Candida (yeast) problem. This questionnaire is not definitive. On its own, it cannot determine with absolute certainty if you have a problem.

Section I: HISTORY

1. Have you taken antibiotics (such as tetracyclines for acne) for two months or longer?	25
2. Have you, at any time in your life taken broad spectrum antibiotic for respiration, urinary or other infection (for more than two months or longer, or 4 or more short courses within a year)?	20
3. Have you ever had a persistent vaginal infection or more than 3 episodes in one year?	25
4. Have you been pregnant two or more times?	5
... one time ?	3
5. Have you ever taken birth control pills for more than two years?	15
... six months, to 2 years?	8
6. Have you ever taken cortisol-type drugs (e.g. prednisone, decadron etc.) for more than two weeks?	15
... two or fewer weeks?	6
7. Do you get a negative response to perfumes, insecticides or chemical?	
... with moderate to severe symptoms?	20
... mild symptoms?	5
8. Does damp day or moldy places make your symptom worse?	25
9. Do you have persistent athletes foot, "jock itch", or other fungus on skin or nails?	
... severe or persistent	25
... mild to moderate	10
10. Do you crave sugar?	15
11. Do you crave bread?	20
12. Do you crave alcoholic beverages?	10
13. Does tobacco smoke **really** bother you?	15
Total points Section I	____

Section II: Major Symptoms

For each symptom which is present, enter the appropriate score:

if mild, ... 3 points
if moderate ... 6 points
if severe ... 9 points

Add the total below

1. Fatigue or lethargy ----
2. Feeling of being "drained" ----
3. Poor memory ----
4. Feeling "spacey" or "unreal" ----
5. Depression ----
6. Numbness, burning or tingling ----
7. Muscle aches and pains ----
8. Muscle weakness or partial paralysis ----
9. Pain and/or swollen joints ----
10. Abdominal bloating or pain ----
11. Constipation ----
12. Diarrhea ----
13. Bloating in general ----
14. Troublesome vaginal discharge ----
15. Persistent vaginal burning or itching ----
16. Enlarged prostate ----
17. Impotency ----
18. Loss of sex drive ----
19. Pelvic inflammatory disease or endometriosis ----
20. Problems with menstrual cycle ----
21. Premenstrual tension ----
22. Spots in front of eyes ----
23. Erratic vision ----

Total for Section II ----

Section III: Other Symptoms

For each symptom which is present, enter the appropriate point value in the column.

If mild	... 1 point
If moderate	... 2 points
If severe or persistent	... 3 points

1. Drowsiness ____
2. Irritability or jitteriness ____
3. Inco-ordination ____
4. Concentration problems ____
5. Mood swings ____
6. Headaches ____
7. Dizziness/vertigo/loss of balance ____
8. Feeling of swollen head or tingling pressure above ears ____
9. Itching ____
10. Rashes ____
11. Heartburn ____
12. Indigestion ____
13. Intestinal gas or belching ____
14. Mucus in stools ____
15. Hemorrhoids ____
16. Dry mouth ____
17. Blisters, cancer or rash in mouth ____
18. Bad breath ____
19. Swollen joints ____
20. Nasal congestion or discharge ____
21. Postnasal drip ____
22. Dry or sore throat ____
23. Nasal itching ____
24. Coughing ____
25. Pain or tightness in chest ____
26. Wheezing or shortness of breath ____
27. Urinary frequency or urgency ____
28. Burning on urination ____
29. Failing vision ____
30. Burning or tearing of eyes ____
31. Recurrent ear infections ____
32. Fluid in ears ____
33. Ear pain or deafness ____
34. Tubes in ears ____
35. Low thyroid ____
36. Other symptoms: ____

Total for Section III ____

Grand Total Score (Add Sections I, II and III) ______

Females

1. If your score is over 175, almost certainly Candida is a contributing factor to your health condition.
2. If your score is over 120, it is likely that Candida is causing some health issues.
3. If your score is between 60-120, Candida possibly contributes to your health but in a minor way.
4. A score less than 60 means that Candida is not causing a problem significant enough to treat.

Males

For males the score is downgraded a bit, with above 100 putting you in category 1; 80-100 category 2; 50-80 category 3 and below 50 categorized as not of any concern.

We start treating females if above 120 and males if above 80.

Candida Symptom Score (Short Questionnaire)

Enter a number (from 0 - 5) after each of the following symptoms related to *Candida*. Zero (0) would represent "not present", 5 would represent very severe expression of the symptom.

Vaginal discharge		_____
Frequent urination		_____
Bladder infections		_____
Sensitivity to smoke, perfume, insecticides, drycleaning fumes, chemical fumes		_____
All symptoms increase in dampness or on muggy days		_____
Athlete's foot, ringworm, "jock itch"		_____
Do you crave	sugar?	_____
"	bread?	_____
"	wine or beer?	_____
"	peanuts?	_____
"	oranges?	_____
"	grapes or raisins?	_____
Fatigue or lethargy		_____
Feeling "drained"		_____
Feeling "spacey" or "unreal"		_____
Depression		_____
Numbness		_____
Abdominal pain		_____
Constipation		_____
Diarrhea		_____
Bloating		_____
Low sex drive		_____
Cramps and/or menstrual irregularities		_____
Spots in front of eyes		_____
Irritability		_____
Inability to concentrate		_____
Mood swings		_____
Headaches		_____
Dizziness/loss of balance		_____
Itching		_____
Rashes		_____
Heartburn		_____
Indigestion		_____
Belching and/or passing gas		_____
Burning anus		_____
Bad breath		_____
Nasal congestion		_____
Burning or tearing of eyes		_____

Total Score on Short Questionnaire _____

(Treatment is recommended if females are above 20 or males are above 15)

Complex Carbohydrate Diet

- No sugar, honey, maple syrup or sweetening agent of any type
- No baked goods - only two slices of bread daily
- No dried fruit - unless soaked overnight and stewed
- All fruit juice diluted (50% with distilled water preferred)
- No food with preservatives
- Little salt
- No alcohol
- Low intake of black tea (maximum of two cups daily)
- Low intake of coffee (maximum of two cups daily)
- Low intake of bananas, potatoes or pasta

Fruit juice or a piece of fresh fruit 1/2 hour before breakfast (optional)

Breakfast Grain (quality as in numbered order)

1. millet
2. buckwheat
3. rye or rice
4. cornmeal
5. seven grain cereal
6. other grains

All of these are prepared like rice and eaten on the savory side. A tasty suggestion is to add engevita yeast and *Dr. Jensen's Vegetable Seasoning* plus some butter or oil.

Morning Snack (mandatory) vegetable sticks, nuts, fruit, yogurt, buttermilk or cottage cheese, and 500 mg Vitamin C.

Lunch The main part of the meal should be a green salad; soup, a sandwich or a vegetable dish can also be eaten.

Afternoon Snack (mandatory) same as morning.

Supper The major part of the meal should be a variety of cooked vegetables. A casserole, grains and/or meat can be added if desired. The addition of a salad is desirable.

Evening Snack (mandatory) same as morning.

Blood Sugar Questionnaire

Enter a number after the symptoms listed below ranging from 0 to 3. Zero (0) represents symptom "not present". Three indicates that the symptom is present in a severe form.

Abnormal craving for sweets	_____
Afternoon headaches	_____
Consume alcohol	_____
Allergies - tendency to asthma, hayfever, rashes	_____
Awaken after a few hours of sleep - unable to get back to sleep	_____
Aware of breathing heavily	_____
Bad dreams	_____
Bleeding gums	_____
Blurred vision	_____
Brown spots or bronzing of skin	_____
Bruise easily, "black and blue spots"	_____
Butterfly stomach, cramps	_____
Can't decide easily	_____
Can't start in morning before coffee	_____
Can't work under pressure	_____
Chronic fatigue	_____
Chronic nervous exhaustion	_____
Convulsions	_____
Crave candy or coffee in afternoon	_____
Depressed	_____
Dizzines, giddiness or lightheadedness	_____
Drink more than 3 cups of coffee or cola daily	_____
Get hungry or feel faint unless eating frequently	_____
Eat when nervous	_____
Fatigue is relieved by eating	_____
Fearful	_____
Get "shaky" when hungry	_____
Hallucinations	_____
Hand tremors (or trembles)	_____
Heart palpitates if hunger is prolonged	_____
Highly emotional	_____
Nibble between meals because of hunger	_____
Insomnia	_____
Irritable before meals	_____
Lack of energy	_____
Magnify insignificant events	_____
Moods of depression, "blues" or melancholy	_____
Poor memory or ability to concentrate	_____
Reduced initiative	_____
Sleepy after meals	_____
Weakness, dizziness	_____
Worrier, feel insecure	_____
Feel better after 10 am snack than before	_____
Symptoms come before breakfast	_____

Total Score -----

A score of less than 20 is within the normal limits. A higher score is presumptive evidence of possible carbohydrate intolerance.

Daily Food Regime

In the Daily Food Regime there are two basic rules that should be followed: variety and food combination.

The food should be as varied as possible. If a person's diet has variety a wide range of vitamins, minerals and other essential nutrients are provided. It is also good to vary the diet according to the season by trying to eat foods that are "in season". In the summer there is abundant fresh fruit and vegetables and this lighter diet feels much better with the hot summer weather. In the winter the diet should be heavier with more grains, proteins, starches, oils and maybe even meat.

A good general diet over a period of a day would contain two different fruits, at least 4 to 6 vegetables, 1 protein and 1 starch, with fruit or vegetable juice between meals if desired. Eat at least two types of leafy green vegetables daily.

One half hour before breakfast drink unsweetened juice. It is good to follow this with at least 12 minutes of aerobic exercise (if not done at this time it should be done some other time during the day).

Breakfast A fruit with a health drink; a grain with a health drink or a protein with a health drink.

Lunch (Lunch and Dinner may be interchanged) Raw salad, one starch and a health drink.

Dinner (Lunch and Dinner may be interchanged) A small raw salad, at least two cooked vegetables, one protein, and a broth or health drink if desired.

Grains Millet, buckwheat, cornmeal, rice, barley, seven grain cereal, Red River cereal, Roman Meal.

Protein

If vegetarian: Beans (preferably sprouted and/or slow cooked), nut butters, tofu, curded dairy (if desired) and high protein vegetables.

If you eat meat: Fish or poultry twice a week, lean meat twice a week, curded dairy once a week, eggs once a week (preferably soft, poached or boiled).

Vegetables Artichokes, asparagus, beans, beets, broccoli, brussel sprouts, cabbage, carrots, cauliflower, cucumber, celery, dandelion, endive, corn, peas, peppers, kale, kohlrabi, lettuce, lotus, okra, sprouts, onions, garlic, parsley, parsnips, pumpkin, radishes, rutabagas, salsify, spinach, squash, swiss chard, turnip, zucchini, tomatoes, avocado, and eggplant.

Starches Baked potato or grain.

Health Drink Vegetable broth, coffee substitute, curded dairy blender drink, herbal tea. Many people feel it is good to have three to seven favorite herbal drinks, rotating them for variety, in a cycle. Some good teas for this are oatstraw, comfrey, alfalfa, mint, parsley, raspberry, grain tea and dandelion root tea.

Food Notes

You should never eat protein and starches or proteins and sweets together. You may wish to trade the evening and noon meals around. It takes exercise to handle raw food and we generally get more exercise after our noon meal. Starches also need exercise so if one eats sandwiches, the time to do so is usually at noon. Fruit can be substituted for any of these meals. If you do not feel hungry or do not feel well, a fruit meal is often the best food to eat.

Rules of Eating

1. If you are not comfortable in mind and body (in pain, emotionally upset, not hungry, chilled, overheated, acutely ill) you should miss the meal.
2. Be sure to chew your food thoroughly.
3. Do not eat beyond your needs.

Three-day Detoxification Diet

This three-day detoxification fast has done wonders for many people, eliminating mucus, chemical and drug deposits, while helping to revitalize the body. (Times given may be varied to suit your schedule, as long as the intervals are maintained).

Day One On arising drink eight ounces of prune juice. In 1/2 hour drink another eight ounces of prune juice. The rest of the day drink as much apple juice as possible, diluted 50/50 with distilled water, until 6:00 P.M.

Take nothing between 6:00 and 9:00 p.m. At 9:00 make and drink the following mixture: juice of two oranges, juice of one lemon, 5 - 10 tablespoons olive oil, 1- 3 cloves of garlic (if desired) finely chopped. Blend in a blender or shake thoroughly. Take nothing else until 8:00 a.m. the next morning.

Day Two Do a warm water enema. Drink eight ounces of prune juice. Start drinking diluted apple juice and repeat day one.

Day Three Repeat day two.

Do not take any vitamins or other supplements during this period unless otherwise stated. Take 2 Lower Bowel Tonic three times daily.

The more apple juice you drink, the more cleansing is accomplished.

Remember, drink slowly!

D-Tox Diet (12 Day)

Four formulas are associated with the D-Tox Diet:

1. Lower Bowel Tonic
2. Cleansing Formula
3. Liver Formula
4. Cleansing Tincture

Suggested Dosage Two tablets (or 20 drops) of each product with both breakfast and supper.

The diet associated with the program is of great importance. During this period, you can eat all you want but the selection of food is quite important. The diet should consist of at least 80% alkaline and neutral ash foods with less than 20%acid ash foods. Referring to the chart on the next page, one should eat less than 20% of the diet from foods in Column 1, with 80% or more of your foods from Columns 2 and 3 combined.

If the food is not listed on this chart, you cannot eat it!

It is strongly recommended that no alcohol is consumed during this program. Although it is best not to drink coffee during this period of time, if it is part of your normal diet, you can drink a maximum of two cups of black coffee per day. Herbals teas are quite acceptable. The addition of spice to the diet is quite alright, but the use of store-bought condiments such as ketchup should be avoided.

Note: There are no breads or other flour products (e.g. breads, cakes, cookies, pastas or the like), dairy products (except butter) or tropical fruit during this program.

One should try to eliminate all foods that might plug up your system during a detox. Your diet does not have to be mundane. Remember that over 95% of the world's population eats these types of foods even today. As a species, humans have had these types of foods for over 99% of our history and even today, most people in the world would consider this diet feasting. Experimenting with foods from other cultures can make the diet delicious and even gourmet.

ACID - ALKALINE - ASH CHART

Eat less than 20% of your diet from this column.

Column 1
Protein Foods
Acid Ash Positive

Most Recommended

Fish (eat all you want even if over 20% of total diet)

Acceptable during Program

Beans (dried)
Beef
Coffee (Black - maximum two cups per day)
Eggs (whole)
Lamb
Lentils
Liver
Most Nuts (except almonds and brazils. See column 2)
Peas (dried)
Poultry
Prunes (cooked)
Rhubarb (cooked)
Rice (white)
Soy Beans
Tea (black)
Veal
Wheat Germ
Whole Grains (most)

Not Recommended during program

Buttermilk
Cheese (natural)
Pork
Seafood (shellfish)
Yogurt

Eat 80% or more of your diet from both columns 2 and 3 combined

Column 2
Starch Foods
Alkaline Ash Negative

Most Recommended

Almonds
Brown Rice
Millet - Buckwheat

Acceptable during Program

Apples
Apricots
Berries
Brazil Nuts
Cherries
Peaches/Pears/Plums
Popcorn
Potatoes (baked)
Pumpkin - Squash
Tomatoes (fresh)

Not Recommended during program

Bananas
Cantaloupe
Currants
Dates and Figs
Flour (white)
Grapes
Honey
Maple Syrup
Melons
Molasses
Pasta (i.e., macaroni, spaghetti)
Pineapple
Raisins
Soups (thick)
Tropical fruit

Not Recommended at any time

Cakes
Candy
Cereal (processed)
Flour gravy
Ice cream
Jams and Jellies
Oily nuts & Peanuts
Pies and Pastries
Sugar (white or brown)

Column 3
Bulk Forming Foods
Neutral Ash

Most Recommended

Chives
Garlic
Onions

Acceptable during Program

Arugula
Artichokes
Asparagus
Avocado
Beets or Beet Tops
Broccoli
Brussel Sprouts
Butter
Cabbage
Carrots
Celery
Collard
Corn
Cucumbers
Dandelion
Eggplant
Endive
Escarole
Green Beans/Green Peas
Green Peppers/Red Peppers
Kale
Kohlrabi
Lettuce
Mustard Greens
Okra
Olive Oil
Parsley
Parsnips
Peppermint
Radicchio
Radishes
Rutabagas
Sorrel
Spinach
Turnips
Water Cress

Not Recommended during program

Cottage cheese
Mushrooms

Breaking a Fast

A fast should be broken slowly! It should take half as long to break the fast as the length of the fast (e.g. five days for a ten day fast).

After a Four-day or less Fast

Day One Eat melons; if unavailable, other juicy fruit, small portions only.

Day Two Fruit for breakfast; raw vegetable salads for the rest of the day, still with small portions.

Day Three At least three days of the Inner Cleanse diet at normal portions.

After Five days and over

Day One Eat a small portion of melon for breakfast. Drink diluted apple, grape or orange juice during the day and a small portion of melon for dinner.

Day Two Eat three fruit meals (small portions); drink fruit juice.

Day Three Fruit for breakfast; raw vegetable salad for the rest of the day. Drink vegetable juice near vegetable meals and fruit juice near fruit meals.

Day Four Start on Inner Cleanse diet and remember that it takes half as long as your fast to get to normal portions.

Inner Cleanse Diet

If you are preceding the Inner Cleanse with a fast, eat small quantities of raw food on the first day, building up to start the full Inner Cleanse diet over a period half as long as your fast, (e.g. for a 10 day fast, take 5 days to reach full proportions).

For the Inner Cleanse diet you will be able to **feast** - not fast! The idea is to fill your body with natural precious vitamins and minerals. When a sufficient amount of these live substances reaches the cells of your body, there will be a cleansing and elimination of toxic material throughout it. This program will be a good start for you to have a strong, healthy body with lots of energy. Follow the directions carefully.

- No dairy products (except where noted), potatoes (yams are OK), avocadoes
- No dried fruit, grains, beans
- No tomatoes, baked goods (except where noted), eggplant
- No sugar, honey, maple syrup or sweetening agent of any type
- No bananas, pasta, preserved food, meat
- No coffee, black tea, or alcohol
- Little salt
- Stop all supplements for duration of Cleanse unless otherwise specified.

Before Breakfast Fifteen minutes before you are ready to eat breakfast, squeeze the juice of a lemon in a medium glass of hot water and drink it.

Breakfast Apple or Grapefruit juice - eight ounces minimum. You can take more if you desire, but be sure that you take at least eight ounces. Yogurt - up to five tablespoons of plain yogurt (if desired). Fresh fruit - one-half pound. You may eat more, but be sure to eat at least one-half pound. (Remember: no bananas or avocadoes)

Lunch Vegetable mineral broth - Drink two cups during the meal. Salad - Make a chopped salad of fresh raw vegetables. Use a dressing of olive oil, lemon juice, kelp or dulse and engevita yeast (if desired). Eat at least eight level tablespoonsful of salad. Use at least four of the following vegetables: artichokes, asparagus, beans, beets, broccoli, brussel sprouts, cabbage, carrots cauliflower, cucumber, celery, dandelion, endive, corn, peas, peppers, kale, kohlrabi, lettuce, lotus, okra, sprouts, onions, garlic, parsley, parsnips, pumpkin, radishes, rutabaga, salsify, spinach, squash, swiss chard, turnip, zucchini.

Dinner Vegetable mineral broth - Drink two cups during the meal. Cooked vegetables - Select three or more of the vegetables listed for lunch and steam or stir fry them in butter. Eat a generous portion. Cooked vegetables are necessary in the evening for proper cleansing. A salad can be added. Bread - One medium slice of whole grain bread with butter (if desired).

Snacks Between meals you should drink all the fruit or vegetable juice you like. You may also eat raw vegetables or fruits. You should allow at least 1/2 hour between eating fruit and eating vegetables. The more live food you can eat or drink, the more cleansing will be done. If fresh fruit juice cannot be obtained, canned varieties from the Health Food store will do. Make the Vegetable Mineral Broth and drink as much as you like.

Vegetable mineral broth

2 cups carrot tops (leaves)
2 cups potato peels, 1/4 inch thick
2 cups beet tops
3 cups celery (stalks and leaves)
2 cups parsley (1 cup dehydrated)

Cover with distilled water and simmer for 20 minutes. Strain, keep broth and discard vegetables. If one of the vegetables is unobtainable, just leave it out. (Replace it with one of the other vegetables if possible.)

You can add garlic, onion or other vegetables and vegetable ends. Some people like to add miso, soya sauce or Dr. Jensen's "Vegetable Broth or Seasoning" in the last few minutes for taste.

Drink hot or cold.

If time is limited you can take one tablespoon of Dr. Jensen's "Vegetable Broth or Seasoning' and pour one cup of boiled water over it as a substitute.

"Lemon Aid" Cleanse

The "Lemon Aid" Cleanse is designed for eliminating toxins and congestion while revitalizing the body. We use this cleanse in some of the longer cleansing programs, for it doesn't create a lack of physical energy even after ten days. In its simplicity it is easy to follow at home, at work or while travelling. The major part of the cleanse is drinking the following mixture:

2 tablespoons of freshly squeezed lemons or limes
1 tablespoon Maple Syrup
1/10 teaspoon Cayenne pepper (more if desired)

Take this mixture and put it in 8 -10 ounces of water, warm or cold. The lemons or limes have to be fresh, not canned; organic ones are best if possible. The maple syrup should be grade B or C, as they are higher in mineral content.

We have found it is sometimes more convenient to make up a days supply at one time. We do this with:

2 cups freshly squeezed lemons
1 cup Maple Syrup
1 or more teaspoons of Cayenne

Of this mixture, take three tablespoonsful per 8 -10 ounce glass.

You should drink between 6 and 12 glasses daily (more if desired). If you also want to lose weight with this program, keep close to six cups daily.

During this cleansing we have to keep the bowel active (to eliminate toxins), so for the first three mornings do an enema with warm water. We also suggest:

2 Lower Bowel Tonic, 3 times daily
(increase if necessary)

During the cleanse, take no vitamins or other supplements unless otherwise specified. Of course no food is taken during this period. For a change, you could drink a cup of mint tea in the evening.

Remember: drink slowly!

Liver Flush

The Liver Flush is a wholesale cleansing of the body and should only be done under a practitioner's care.

This Liver Flush is best preceded with one month of liver herbs such as Liver Formula (two capsules, three times daily) and/or the Three Day Detoxification Fast.

In the morning do an enema or colonic; one half-hour later drink eight ounces of prune juice. Drink diluted apple juice only (mixed half and half with distilled water) until 6:00 p.m. Don't take in anything until 9:00 p.m.

At that time measure out:

1-1 1/2 cups pure olive oil (cold pressed)
1- 1 1/2 cups freshly squeezed lemon juice

Take three tablespoons of each; wait 15 minutes and repeat until finished (about three hours). Try not to stop even if you become nauseated or vomit. Try to continue until you are finished, as you are performing a thorough cleansing of toxins and mucus.

When you are ready to go to bed, sleep on your right side, to put slight pressure on the liver.

If you wake up very nauseated and feel you can't go on, and ONLY if you can't go on, take one tablespoon of pure gelatin, rinse your mouth with water and go back to sleep. This will completely stop the action of the cleanse.

In the morning, do two enemas or preferably have a colonic.

Mucusless Diet

Foods that are most likely to cause mucus in the system are dairy and flour. Other foods like highly processed food, excessive red meat might also contribute to mucus content. A mucusless diet consist of no dairy, flour or processed food. You can usually eat the whole grains but not the flours of the grain. This should be adopted strictly for 2 months. After this amount of time, dairy or flour can be introduced into the diet 1-2 times per week.

The Ultimate Weight Loss Program

This weight loss program doesn't just help you lose weight that you will gain back a week later. This is a program which aids in adjusting the "idle" of your metabolic rate. Your body will start to burn up fat, changing weight into muscle, thereby not only reducing bulk but making you more shapely. So let's start with shaping up and keeping fit!

Breakfast 2 tablespoons of Psyllax (in a liquid), 2 tablespoons of Protein Powder (in a liquid), 1 Multivitamins and minerals.

Lunch 1 tablespoon Psyllax, 2 tablespoons Protein Powder, 1 Multivitamins and minerals.

Eat a bowl of clear vegetable soup made from non-starchy vegetables.

Supper 2 tablespoons Psyllax, 2 tablespoons Protein Powder, 1 Multivitamins and minerals

Eat a salad of non-starchy vegetables.

Lunch and Supper can be exchanged.

Drink at least 12 cups of fluid during the day. The Psyllax tastes best in tomato juice. Any liquid may be used with the Protein Powder.

Do at least 15 minutes of aerobic exercise daily.

The diet must be done for more than five days to be effective and not more than twenty days followed by a ten-day break, and repeated if desired.

Questions and Answers

Should vitamins and minerals be used together with herbs?

I feel that vitamins, minerals, herbs, diet, exercise, and mental and emotional attitudes are all part of a wholistic healing program and cannot be separated. If you were building a brick house, you might want a forklift or bulldozer to help you lift the bricks into place. In building this foundation we can liken the bricks to minerals as they are building blocks of the body. Vitamins are similar to the gasoline used to run the bulldozer (vitamins often work as co-enzymes to activate enzymes) and the bulldozer itself is like the body's enzymes that catalyze actions in the body. Now, we **could** build a house with these few substances, but a simple house it would be! If we were then to add herbs (which also contain vitamins, minerals, enzymes and other substances) to our own building program, it would be similar to adding a foreman to the construction project. Now we can create a house with a few fancy trimmings! Because of the cleansing nature of herbs we are even left with some workers to clean and tidy up the mess after the building is complete.

Many would say at this point, "If herbs are so good, why not use them alone." Herbs, like vitamins and minerals, may be used alone. The best and fastest results, however, are obtained when all of the raw materials for the construction are already in the form required for that construction. By using all three together you have all the parts present right at the start of the building, without having to spend time and energy recycling used parts to get the other raw materials needed. This is especially important because some of those "used parts", which were recycled are used later in the building process in their original form!

So, not only should we combine vitamins, minerals and herbs, we should be careful to include exercise, diet, and mental/emotional attitudes in our building process.

How many herbal formulas should a person use at the same time?

In general, I would say that a person should not be working on more than four areas of the body at one time. Of course, as with every rule, there are exceptions. A woman may be working on one area, female organs for example, but will be using a Female Formula and Vitamin E. This constitutes only one problem area, and the woman may work on up to three other organs or tissues at the same time. The number of **formulas** then depends on the nature of the individual problems.

Are there any herbal formulas that should not be used with other herbal formulas?

Specific information as to the combinations involved would provide the most accurate answer. As with medical drugs, certain herbs do not combine well, and it is a general practice not to work on diverse areas of the body at exactly the same time. If you were working on the heart and the colon, the best results would be obtained by taking the formulas at different times of day, say at breakfast and lunch. If you try to work on two areas at the same time, the vital energies of the body are pulled in two different directions, giving less power for healing in both areas. If, however, you were dealing with the pancreas, liver and large intestine, then there is a vast difference: all are related to the digestive system so the energy being applied is kept localized.

How long does one have to use herbs relative to vitamins?

When using herbal formulas we are dealing with a more definite time period than for the use of vitamins. If a formula were being used for kidneys, we would continue use until the organ built up its strength, usually a period of three to nine months (more in some cases). Vitamins, though, are chemicals necessary for life support that are not produced in the body in sufficient quantity to maintain it. Because of this vitamins must be consumed regularly throughout our lives either in our diet or in pill form. Many of these vitamin needs can be supplied from our diet, but the vitamin content of the foods we eat is deteriorating and the stress of the modern world is placing a larger vitamin demand on us. This is where vitamin supplements may make the difference.

Herbs are used as a relatively short-term tool and the need for them lasts only as long as the problem exists. Once the healing is done, and as long as we keep from the habits that gave us the problems in the first place, the herbs may no longer be needed.

Where should I start if I want to go on a herbal program?

Each health program is highly individualized, but it is usual to begin at the digestive system. If this system is not working adequately, there will be inefficient absorption of the nutrients, herbs and vitamins that are taken to help other systems and organs of the body.

What would be a step-by-step program for building up the body?

After cleansing the digestive system to permit more efficient use of the nutrients supplied, we usually move to work on the eliminatory organs: colon, kidneys, lungs and skin. With these systems operating well we can remove toxin buildup inside the body. At this time, too, we can start to build the other specific vital areas of the individual that require attention. These would include the heart, liver, endocrine glands and nervous system. From this point we would start to concentrate on less vital areas.

What is a healing crisis?

The concept of the "healing crisis" is found in a Homeopathic Law called Hering's Law of Cure, which states that all cure comes from within out, from the head down and in the reverse order of the appearance of the symptoms.

Let us take the example of a person who goes to a drugstore upon "catching" a cold. The product purchased is one advertised to relieve the symptoms of a cold. This product will likely relieve the symptoms of the cold, but it probably won't do much more that is beneficial. It will, in all likelihood, dry up and crystallize the mucus and toxins being released through the action of the cold, driving them deeply into the bronchial tissues. This changes the condition from acute to subacute, a less noticeable state, making the person feel better. Some time later (often at the change of a season) the body will make its attempt to throw these toxins off. This may result in a cold, cough or even the flu, which frequently drives the person back to the time-tested formula used earlier to relieve the "problem". This, of course, reverses the cleansing at once, driving the mucus and toxins ever more deeply into the tissues. Starting with a cold, a usual history is to develop tendencies to coughs, flus, bronchitis or hayfever, then asthma and finally, perhaps, a degenerate and chronically diseased lung.

At some stage, however, the person may decide to begin living in a more healthy manner and eventually begins to feel better. This healthy period progresses happily until the person is usually heard to remark, "haven't felt this good in years". At this point the body has built up enough strength again so that it attempts once more to eliminate some of the toxins. In our example the person might appear to "catch" asthma, which he hasn't had for years. During this crisis, the body is simply trying to rid itself of the toxins and the disharmonies.

Throughout a cleansing/building program there will be periods of better health punctuated by short crises. The person in our example will then, over perhaps months or years, re-experience asthma, hayfever, bronchitis, flus, coughs and colds, in that order. Each of these conditions will appear as a Healing Crisis, with symptoms similar to that of the original disease crisis. The major difference is that the crisis is of much shorter duration and is often more dramatic. The person also feels much better both before and after the crisis (if left to run its natural course). The individual should ensure the intake of plenty of vitamins, minerals, herbs specific to the problem and brothy soups to promote a speedy recovery.

Glossary of Herbal Terms

Alterative Producing a healthful change without perception.
Anodyne Relieves mild pain.
Anthelmintic A medicine that expels worms.
Antibilious Acts on the bile, relieving biliousness.
Antiemetic Stops vomiting.
Antiperiodic Preventing regular recurrences.
Antilithic Prevents the formation of stones in the urinary organs.
Antirheumatic Relieves or cures rheumatism.
Antiscorbutic Cures or prevents scurvy.
Antiseptic A medicine that prevents putrefaction.
Antispasmodic Relieves or prevents spasms.
Antisyphilitic Having effect of curing or relieving syphilis.
Aperient Gently laxative without purging.
Aromatic A stimulant, spicy, anti-griping.
Astringent Causes contraction and arrests discharges.
Carminative Expels wind from the bowels.
Cathartic Evacuates the bowels (a purgative).
Cephalic Pertaining to the head.
Cholagogue Increases the flow of bile into the intestine.
Condiment Improves the flavor of foods.
Demulcent Soothing, relieves inflammation, especially for skin and mucous membranes.
Deobstruent Removes obstruction.
Depurative Purifies the blood.
Detergent Cleansing.
Diaphoretic Produces perspiration.
Discutient Dissolves and heals tumors.
Diuretic Increases the secretion and flow of urine.
Emetic Produces vomiting.
Emmenagogue Promotes menstruation.
Emollient Softens and soothes inflamed parts when locally applied.
Esculent Edible.
Exanthematous Pertaining to skin eruptions and diseases.
Expectorant Facilitates expulsion of mucus or phlegm from the lungs and throat.
Febrifuge Abates and reduces fevers.
Hepatic Pertaining to the liver.
Laxative Promotes bowel action.

Lithotriptic Dissolves calculi (stones) in the urinary organs.

Mucilaginous Soothing to all inflammations.

Nauseant Produces vomiting.

Nervine Acts specifically on the nervous system, stops nervous excitement, tonic.

Parturient Induces and promotes labor at childbirth.

Pectoral A remedy for chest afflictions.

Refrigerant Cooling.

Resolvent Dissolves boils, tumors, and other inflammations.

Rubefacient Increases circulation and produces red skin.

Sedative Quiets nerve action and promotes sleep.

Sialogogue Increases the secretion of saliva.

Stomachic Excites the action of the stomach, has the effect of strengthening it and relieving indigestion.

Styptic Arrests hemorrhage.

Sudorific Produces profuse perspiration.

Tonic A remedy which is invigorating, strengthening, and toning.

Vermifuge Expels worms from the intestines.

Index

*Correspondence Courses * Classroom Courses*

Wild Rose College of Natural Healing, Calgary Alberta

Since its inception by Terry Willard in 1975, the Wild Rose College of Natural Healing has been offering a broad range of workshops and courses to individuals interested in the healing arts. The expanding responsibility for self-health has generated much interest in the college over the last 20 years. The staff are proud to play a part in the trend toward preventative health and "well-being" awareness.

Wild Rose is a centre for the casual and the serious student to learn introductory biological sciences in addition to a broad range of complementary therapies, techniques and natural health concepts. Each of the courses emphasizes wholism of the individual - the integration of body, mind and spirit.

The dramatic increase in interest in wholistic medicine in the last few years has made a career in this area very attractive. To satisfy demand, the college has two diploma programs available through correspondence. For Canadian students, the Wholistic Therapist Diploma program is now the minimum requirement for a herbalist/health practitioner. For U.S. and international students, both the **Master Herbalist** and **Wholistic Therapist** diploma programs are available. Correspondence courses may be started at any time and completed at a comfortable pace established by the student, subject to a maximum of one year for each course.

A number of courses are available through classroom instruction on weekday evenings, with some weekeday "intensives" and workshops on the weekends.

Credit from correspondence courses is transferable into the classroom programs in both Calgary and Vancouver.

For additional information and enquiries contact the college co-ordinator at:

Wild Rose College of Natural Healing
400, 1228 Kensington Rd. N.W.
Calgary, Alberta, Canada, T2N 4P9
Telephone: (403) 270-0936 Fax: (403) 283-0799

Classroom Courses

Coastal Mountain College of Healing Arts, Vancouver, British Columbia, Canada

In September 1995, the Wild Rose College of Natural Healing in Vancouver, B.C., changed its name to Coastal Mountain College of Healing Arts. This college has daytime, evening and weekend classes and incorporated a variety of diploma programs which include **Clinical Herbalist**, **Practical Herbalist** and **Wholistic Counselling Practitioner**.

The **Clinical Herbalist** program encompasses several disciplines of healing through classroom instruction, in addition to 400 hours of supervised clinical practicum. Designed for the serious student of herbal medicine, the program extends over three years and may be taken full- or part-time.

The **Wholistic Counselling Practitioner** program combines the latest in clinical counselling theories and approaches along with a wide range of wholistic and transpersonal counselling perspectives. Skills are developed through a series of practica, clinical supervision opportunities and field placements. The program is divided into three 10-week trimesters per year for three years.

Designed for people who want to go into the business of herbs, the **Practical Herbalist** Diploma program blends the scientific background needed by a professional herbalist with practical work experiences that provide a solid foundation upon which to build a career as a grower, wildcrafter, manufacturer, distributor, wholesaler or retailer. It is a one year course consisting of two full-time semesters.

Through the Continuing Education department, the college offers a broad range of programs during evenings and weekends: from wholistic therapies and bodywork to introductory herbology and wildcrafting.

Our philosophy has been to merge traditional natural healing arts with modern scientific methods to educate the serious student/practitioner and increase public awareness of preventative medicine and natural health practices.

Course calendars can be acquired by contacting:

Coastal Mountain College of Healing Arts,
1745 West 4th Avenue, Vancouver, B.C., V6J 1M2
Telephone: (604) 734-4596   Fax: (604) 734-4597

Other Books written by Terry Willard, Ph.D.

Textbook of Modern Herbology (Second Edition)

A first year text for the aspiring herbalist, *The Textbook of Modern Herbology* is the basis for the Introductory Herbology course at the Wild Rose College of Natural Healing. The *Textbook* integrates human physiology, botany, biology and herbal lore to provide a solid foundation for future study. (400 pp., hard cover)

Wild Rose Scientific Herbal (Second Edition)

For the practicing herbalist or the serious student, the *Wild Rose Scientific Herbal* integrates the information of a entire herbal library under a single cover. Over 125 herbs are described, illustrated and discussed. Information from modern phytochemistry is thoughtfully blended with the traditional energetic descriptions of traditional Chinese and Ayurvedic medicine. (416 pp., hard cover)

Textbook of Advanced Herbology

The culmination of a decade of research, the Textbook is a brand new kind of reference - a review of the biochemical families of herbal constituents from the herbalist's perspective. The reader is introduced to basic chemistry and then to the families or groups of active chemical constituents found in plants. Each chapter contains a "mini-materia medica" which ties medicinal plants to the particular chemical family. Extensively illustrated and indexed. A required text at herbal colleges in several parts of the world.(436 pp., hard cover)

Reishi Mushroom: Herb of Spiritual Potency and Medical Wonder

An exciting account of Dr. Willard's search for the elusive truth about Reishi mushroom, long a revered herb in the Orient. The reader follows Terry from mainland China to the coastal rain forest of British Columbia and finally into the modern clinics of North America. Fully referenced with both modern biochemical research and ancient folklore -- the new standard on this herb in the English language. (167 pp.)

Edible and Medicinal Plants of the Rocky Mountains

Designed as a practical field guide, *Edible and Medicinal Plants of the Rocky Mountains* is richly illustrated with over 200 line drawings and colour photographs to make identification easier. The reader is given botanical, medicinal, culinary and traditional uses for over 150 beautiful plants of western U.S. and Canada. From horsetail soap to currant jam, from alfalfa to yucca, follow a Master Herbalist through one of North America's most breathtaking areas. (colour photos, line drawings, 288pp., reinforced softcover)

FAX / Mail Order Form

FAX to: .... (403) 283-0799
Mail to: .... Wild Rose College of Natural Healing
400 1228 Kensington Rd. N.W.
Calgary, Alberta
T2N 4P9
Voice: .... (403) 270-0936

Textbook of Modern Herbology (2nd Edition)	$65.00	______
Wild Rose Scientific Herbal (2nd Edition)	$65.00	______
Textbook of Advanced Herbology	$65.00	______
Reishi Mushroom: Herb of Spiritual Potency and Medical Wonder	$20.50	______
Edible and Medicinal Plants of the Rocky Mountains	$25.00	______
Wild Rose College Calendar	$3.00	______
Shipping and Handling ($3.00 for first item, plus $1.00 for each additional item except calendar)		______
G.S.T. on subtotal (Canadian orders only)	7%	______
Total value of order		☐

PLEASE PRINT

Name: ______________________________

Street Address: ______________________________

City: ______________ State or Province: ______________

Country: ______________ Postal or ZIP Code: ______________

METHOD OF PAYMENT Money Order ☐ Personal Cheque ☐

VISA/MC # ______________ Exp. Date: ______________

Signature ______________________________

Please note: for orders outside Canada and the United States, payment is in U.S. funds.